ADULT LEARNING

R. BERNARD LOVELL

First published 1979
by Croom Helm Ltd

Reprinted by Croom Helm 1982, 1984 and 1987

Reprinted by Routledge 1989, 1992
11 New Fetter Lane, London EC4P 4EE
29 West 35th Street, New York, NY 10001

Printed and bound in Great Britain by
Biddles Ltd, Guildford and King's Lynn

British Library Cataloguing in Publication Data

Lovell, R. Bernard
    Adult learning — (New patterns of learning series).
    1. Learning, Psychology of
    I. Title II. Series
    153.1′5 BF 318

ISBN 0–415–03693–3

ADULT LEARNING

CONTENTS

To my parents
and
Anna, Rebecca and Jessica

ACKNOWLEDGEMENTS

There are a number of people who have contributed to the writing of this book and I would like to take this opportunity of acknowledging their assistance.

My colleagues in the Psychology Section at Garnett College have contributed in more ways than I can enumerate by sharing their thoughts and ideas about adult learning with me over the years. The staff of the Garnett College library have given me invaluable help by promptly locating and obtaining journal articles and books. Without the help of Margaret Kahan and Barbara Osborne this book would still be pages of near illegible manuscript. They have spent long hours interpreting and on occasions improving upon the manuscript and typing and checking the text. To them both I owe an especial debt of thanks.

Author's Note

There are many nouns used in this book such as 'adult', 'learner', 'individual', 'subject' etc. which are not sex specific. Throughout the book the convention has been adopted of using the male form of the pronoun to represent a member of either sex. I hope this will not be interpreted as sexism but merely as an aid to clarity of expression.

THE COMPLEX NATURE OF ADULT LEARNING

Introduction

This is a book about adult learning and some of the factors that can influence it. Adulthood is the time when the basic skills and abilities, which were so rapidly acquired in childhood, are consolidated and exploited to the full and many new skills and competences are learned. The early chapters of the book are concerned with the mechanisms and processes of adult learning. Many factors can influence the way in which an adult approaches a new learning experience. Some relate to the characteristics of the learner and range from personality and cognitive style to individual differences in age, experience, motivation and self-perception. Others relate to the social context within which the learning takes place and to the way in which any formal teaching is planned, carried out and evaluated. Subsequent chapters deal with these areas.

All adult learners are unique — we are very much the product of our past life. Our present behaviour is largely the consequence of our past learning. Indeed learning is sometimes defined as the process which leads to relatively permanent changes in our potential for performance as the result of our past interaction with the environment. It would be possible to write this book as a series of case-studies illustrating the way in which a limited number of adult learners had assimilated new ideas and skills into their already existing repertoire of behaviour and to try to come to an understanding of the processes of adult learning in this way. However, this approach would be of only limited use to the teacher or administrator faced with attempting to foster the learning of large numbers of unique individuals each with different past learning experiences and backgrounds. For this book to be useful to people engaged in the business of fostering learning it must attempt to make generalisations both about the nature and progress of adult learning and about those factors, internal and external to the learner, which are likely to advance his development.

There are, however, very real problems in trying to generalise about adult learning. To begin with, what are we to understand by adult? Adulthood is one phase in the human life cycle but it is a phase that covers a very lengthy section of the life span. It is a phase that sees the individual pass through many stages in biological, psychological and environmental terms. Adulthood is part of a continuing process. What we were in the past very largely determines what we are now and this in its turn will very largely determine what we will become.

Learning and the Stages of Life

Let us then look briefly at the successive stages of the juvenile and adult phases of human life. Life starts for the individual, at conception, with the fertilisation of the ovum. Roughly 38 weeks from conception, after a period of embryonic and foetal development, he is ready for life outside the womb. The new born infant is largely helpless and totally dependent for survival on the adults in his environment but he rapidly develops competence in the interrelated areas of perception, thought and activity. His rate of learning at this stage is prodigious and it is shaped in innumerable ways by the context in which he is growing up. He may already have developed feelings, about how much trust he can place in the behaviour of others, for example, that may stay with him into adult life. A genetically regulated programme controls the physical development of the individual but this development is also influenced by the environmental and social conditions he encounters. The physical changes which are undergone lead the individual to an increase in competence and to the successful learning of new behaviour. Each newly acquired competence becomes the foundation for subsequent development.

Some time between the ages of about 11 to 16 years the individual develops primary and secondary sexual characteristics. The onset of puberty leads to a host of biological, social and psychological changes for the individual. Once again the patterns for many adult forms of behaviour are established. By the age of 16 years the main programme of genetically regulated growth is coming to an end for most; the child has now become more adult in both appearance and behaviour. Society acknowledges these changes by according the individual certain legal rights and responsibilities. For many secondary education comes to an end.

Sixteen to Twenty Years

The age group 16 to 20 years marks the transition from the juvenile to the adult phase. As he progresses through these years, the individual takes on an adult role in more and more ways. For the purposes of this book we will consider this period to be part of adulthood. For those who are still engaged in formal learning the emphasis now, in both education and training settings, has shifted towards fitting the individual more specifically for an adult occupational role. Socially the individual is engaged in making a shift from the largely dependent status of the juvenile phase to the largely independent status of the adult phase. Often, particularly in urban, industrial communities, the pressure on the individual to change his role and to seek out a new identity for himself during this stage, leads to the adoption of unstable and sometimes deviant behaviour. It is at this time that the individual is most likely to engage in anti-social behaviour; but it is also the time when individuals are often at their most adventurous, creative, socially concerned and idealistic.

Twenty to Twenty-five Years

As the years pass by the individual moves unequivocally into the adult phase of his life. As with the juvenile phase, the biological, social and psychological aspects of behaviour are closely interwoven, but during the adult phase the biological changes have a slow, cumulative effect; with the exception of the menopause there are no clear-cut landmarks. Apart from serious illnesses, which may affect some individuals, there are no rapid biological changes comparable with puberty in their physical, social and psychological effects until the onset of old age. The stages of the adult phase seem most appropriately defined in social terms and because of the different social circumstances of different individuals these stages, and their descriptions are rather more arbitrary.

During early adulthood, say from about 20 to 25 years, the individual is still completing his transition from juvenile to adult status. This is the phase in most societies when the individual begins to be treated as a fully fledged adult. By the end of this period most people in urban industrial societies have completed their preparations for their adult occupational roles and have begun to establish themselves in their work. Most have married and begun to raise a family.

Plainly there are considerable differences in the way in which individuals live their lives. Many women at this stage will be at home learning how best to cope with bringing up young children, some will be pursuing a career. People from different socio-economic circumstances and with differing cultural backgrounds will have varying experiences, but in the main, this is a period when people become more fully involved in a range of formal and informal social activities. The complex network of interrelated social groupings of which the individual finds himself a member influences him and in its turn is influenced by him. During early adulthood many people will still be engaged in formal further and higher education and in occupational training. Physically the individual is at the peak of his powers and as a result of training and practice some will achieve outstanding performances in athletics and sport during this stage. As a consequence of previous learning in the intellectual sphere enough experience has been acquired for some individuals to begin to make significant contributions in the fields of science, art and literature.

Twenty-five to Forty Years

The transition to middle adulthood is a gradual one, marked more by social and economic changes than by other landmarks. The period we are now talking about occurs roughly between the ages of 25 to 40 years, but as we have already noted there are no clear-cut landmarks and these ages are arbitrary ones, appropriate to some individuals but by no means all. For most individuals this period sees the consolidation of both the private and occupational roles. By now he has accumulated a range of material possessions and has established a network of stable social relationships. During this period, depending on the individual's circumstances, he is likely to have continued to make progress in his occupation and in the other spheres of life. Most individuals have plenty of energy for all their interests and responsibilities during this period and much is likely to be achieved. The experience that has been amassed will often be acknowledged by an increase in status and prestige in comparison with early adult status and for many this acknowledgement brings economic security. Attached to this change in status will be the necessity to learn new administrative and social skills. Many women during this period find themselves free to become more fully involved in social and occupational activities outside the home as the children of the family grow up. Some women will now undertake a period of formal training before they enter into their new roles. Physically and intellectually individuals may still appear to be at the height of their powers. There will, however, be some slight deterioration in performance during the period which can be detected if they are pushed to the limits of their capabilities.

Forty to Sixty Years

Late adulthood, or as it is more commonly called 'middle age', covers the period from 40 to 60 years. This is a period when the socio-economic and sex role differences make it even more difficult to generalise usefully about the typical individual. For women the menopause provides an obvious physiological landmark but for most women it does not have social or psychological consequences comparable with the onset of reproductive life at puberty. During this stage the children of the family are likely to leave home and this social change will lead to some readjustments in the way time and material resources are utilised. For some there will be further consolidation of status and position in both public and occupational life; for others will come the realisation that no further progress will be made. For many individuals this is a period when past and present are reassessed, values and attitudes modified and the self-concept revised. Physically there is a lowering of the individual's resources and capabilities during this period; minor ailments may become more frequent and the effects of an unhealthy life style may become more apparent by speeding the process of ageing.

Pre-retirement and Retirement

In the five years leading up to retirement the rate at which the effects of ageing become apparent seems to accelerate for many individuals. There is a sharp jump in the number of individuals who become physically and mentally ill during this period. In situations which push people close to the limits of their physical or intellectual capacity there is a very noticeable decline in competence. During this period some individuals come to hold eminent positions in their social or occupational spheres because they have a wealth of long experience that they can draw upon. In the last year or two before retirement many people consciously 'disengage' themselves from their occupational setting and prepare themselves for the leisure they anticipate lies ahead and for the reduced circumstances they will probably find themselves in. Many do this by attending pre-retirement courses and evening classes and by developing and expanding old interests and pursuits.

Retirement means very different things to people depending upon the individual's sex, socio-economic status and psychological make-up. For men especially it means leaving their main occupation behind and taking to new daily activities. This period often sees a change in people's social interaction and in their standard of living. For many, who have viewed themselves in the past very much in terms of their occupational role and status, it is a difficult time emotionally, necessitating a redefinition of their view of themselves. During this period there is a cumulative decline in abilities as a result of ageing. For some it will be a slow, steady progression; each year will see a slight lowering of capabilities. For others the effects of a serious illness may lead to a rapid diminution in their ability to cope with the affairs of everyday life. As this final stage progresses social involvement with friends and relations assumes more and more significance for most people. The range of activities in which the individual can easily engage will narrow to a very few and these may be of considerable importance in maintaining the individual's morale.

This crude outline of the phases of juvenile and adult life bears some resemblance to the experiences of many living in an urban industrial society. One thing is clear, in each of the stages that have been outlined the individual will be drawing upon and exploiting learning which he has carried out at earlier stages. It is also clear that each stage makes fresh demands upon the individual to learn so that there is never a time when learning is completed.

Age and Approaches to Learning

Although adults are likely to go on learning throughout the whole of their lives, it is certainly true that during the juvenile phase we do have a particular facility for rapid learning and this is acknowledged in all industrialised societies by making formal educational provision for the young available in schools. It is during this juvenile phase that the basic foundations for our subsequent learning are laid down. There is little learning in adulthood that is as important and fundamental as learning to use language and number. Even in the area of sensori-motor skills the facility for learning seems to be far greater during the juvenile phase. Few people who have first come to a musical instrument such as the piano or violin after the age of 13 have gone on to become outstanding performers. Adulthood is the phase when we explore and exploit to the full the implications and the applications of the fundamental learning that we so rapidly acquired in childhood.

From the age composition of classes in further and higher education it can be seen that their popularity is markedly skewed towards the younger end of the age scale with only a small number of people in their fifties or sixties enrolled. If the reasons for attendance at classes are examined the older students tend to fall into two groups. There are those who have been attending some sort of class for years and regard it as part of their normal social activity and then there are those, in most instances the larger group, who have come to the class to increase their skill and knowledge in an area where they already have some expertise. Very few older students go in for courses that lead to a formal examination of their competence. One writer (Jones,

1969), considering the reasons why people attend adult education classes, has distinguished between the 'motive to attend' and the 'motive to learn'. Many mature women attending formal classes give as their main reason for attending 'to get away from home for a few hours'. Many students applying to join a beginners' class in Classical Greek were not interested in learning the language as such, but rather in seeing whether they could cope with learning a language which they considered to be the mark of the fully educated person. Whilst there may often be socio-economic factors that discourage people from undertaking formal learning in middle adulthood, there is good evidence to confirm that reluctance to engage in formal learning does increase with age (Belbin, 1965).

In industry mature adults are reluctant to take up opportunities for retraining whether it is provided by government agencies or private companies. In training schemes that have not been specifically designed for people in middle and late adulthood comparisons of training records almost invariably show the older trainee performing at a lower level than his younger colleague (Shooter *et al.*, 1956). On operations that involve a high degree of manual dexterity, learning efficiency has been shown to fall considerably by the age of 25. When mature adults do take part in retraining programmes, fewer successfully complete the course than would be expected if they were in early adulthood (Newsham, 1969).

The Range of Adult Learning

Formal Learning

Recognising then that there is a much greater participation in formal learning by people in the early stages of adulthood, let us now look at part of the enormous range of learning that adults may undertake. To begin with there are those who are learning in a formal context of some kind; normally there is some special setting such as a class-room, a workshop or a laboratory in which the learning is undertaken. There is a teacher who is in some way responsible for directing the learner's progress and there is some formal syllabus or programme which the learner is following. In this category are all the universities, the polytechnics, institutes of higher education, colleges of education, technical colleges and colleges of further education. Many of the courses in these settings are intended to equip students for their future occupational roles; in some cases considerable further vocational preparation will be necessary before the individual is fully prepared to take up an occupation.

Many of the agencies concerned with the provision of formal learning opportunities for adults are more overtly occupational in their orientation than those we have considered so far. Many people engage in occupational training through the agency of bodies such as the industrial training boards, the Training Services Agency of the Manpower Services Commission, training facilities provided by individual industries or companies or the armed forces. Others engage in formal learning in settings such as adult education institutes, short courses in residential colleges and in commercially run schools and academies. Sometimes this learning has an occupational bias, but often people undertake this kind of formal learning in order to increase their competence and pleasure in other areas of their lives. Some formal adult learning is undertaken in order to help the individual function more effectively in very basic ways. Ante-natal clinics, rehabilitation units in hospitals, sheltered workshops, literacy schemes and special provisions made by social service departments are all examples.

Other formal learning provision is offered on a more entrepreneurial basis, often involving individual tuition in very specialised contexts; many people undertake courses in driving, others arrange to be instructed or coached in sporting and other recreational activities many of which involve the mastery of new physical skills. Other skills such as those required for effective performance in music and the arts are also sometimes studied in settings where the teacher and the student work together on a one to one basis.

Incidental Learning

Besides the formal learning that adults undertake there is an even greater amount of learning of an incidental kind that comes about as a consequence of a person's everyday experiences. There are innumerable ways in which we learn and amass new ideas, facts, attitudes and skills as the result of our day to day interaction with our environment. Work is a major source of incidental learning. Parenthood brings with it a myriad of new things that need to be learnt — how to change a nappy, sterilise a bottle, recognise the symptoms of chicken pox, or choose the right size clothes for a 3-year-old. Social, economic and technological changes all present us with new incidental learning: ten years ago few adults would have known how to operate a cassette tape-recorder or a pocket calculator; in the future many of us will learn how to operate video tape-recorders and home based information retrieval systems and the other products of the silicon chip age.

A great deal of incidental learning comes about through doing; the D.I.Y. enthusiast works out a better way to paint a window frame through the process of trial and error; the gardener notices that roses do better in one part of the garden rather than another. Changes in our life force us to come into contact with parts of the law of which we were previously ignorant and as a result we perhaps learn more about our legal rights and obligations. Sometimes the necessity for incidental learning has been foreseen by others. Instructional leaflets and publicity material can help us learn how to operate a new purchase or how to find our way around the transport system of a foreign country. Sometimes our incidental learning may help us to understand the responses and motivations of others better; sometimes we come to modify our attitudes and values as a result of our day to day experiences.

Even though the above lists seem long, they are very far from complete. If we were to look in detail at what takes place in any of these formal or informal learning situations we would find that many different kinds of learning may be involved. Consider for a moment the variety of learning that would be undertaken by a chiropodist in training. Most obviously there are the manipulative skills that are necessary to carry out the delicate and precise operations on the patient's feet. But before these skills can be appropriately used there are a range of diagnostic skills that must be called into play. Often the diagnosis of the physical condition of the feet requires an understanding of the structure and functioning of the whole body, so a range of medical and biological knowledge must be acquired. For some conditions appliances must be made, so much must be learned about the construction and application of the various appliances and of the materials from which they are made.

Social skills are required to put the patient at his ease and to give advice and guidance in a way that is likely to be heeded. There are also organisational and administrative skills that need to be acquired so that the chiropodist can efficiently organise his work load and make an effective contribution to the smooth functioning of the organisation within which he will work.

Categories of Adult Learning

Although there is such a disparate range of learning tasks which adults are liable to undertake it does seem possible to categorise this learning under a limited number of headings. Perhaps the most obvious is the reception of information; for instance, the chiropodist will learn factual information about the structure of the body, about medicine and so on. In an incidental learning context, a volunteer worker in the Citizen's Advice Bureau will learn factual information about the mass of legislation that affects daily life. Both will also learn a whole range of strategies. In the case of the chiropodist there are strategies to carry out when making a diagnosis, strategies connected with conducting a clinic or looking up the results of previous research. The C.A.B. volunteer will learn strategies connected with interviewing and strategies for helping clients tackle a vast spectrum of problems.

The chiropodist in particular will also have to learn to become proficient in a range of sensori-motor skills. Both the chiropodist and the C.A.B. worker will be involved with the social learning required to set patient or client at their ease, to communicate effectively with others and to internalise the professional values and standards of the group that they have joined.

Aspects of Memory

In later chapters we will go on to explore in more detail the way adults assimilate new information, strategies, skills and social behaviour; we will next consider some aspects of memory and then, in Chapter 2, look at some of the theories of learning advanced by psychologists. All learning, in whatever category it is included, implies the reception of new information, its retention over a period of time and its subsequent recall. To understand more fully what is involved when new material is memorised, we need to consider the stages through which the new information is processed as it progresses from an immediate sensory experience to long-term storage and also the types or levels of analysis that the material seems to go through.

The Stages of Memory

The senses — eyes, ears and other receptors such as those for smell, taste, touch and body posture, receive information which is turned into electro-chemical energy that is then transmitted to the brain via the nervous system. In the brain this information is analysed into forms suitable for storage in the memory. Psychological experiments suggest the possibility that there are three stages to the memorisation process: a sensory memory, a short-term memory and a long-term memory. The physiological aspects of memory are only very partially understood; our memories seem to be distributed across large areas of our brain (Gregg, 1975).

The new material being received, into whichever of our categories it falls, may be analysed at different levels. For example, if we are driving to work listening to a radio discussion we may be processing the information to a high level, carefully attending to every point that is made so that we have a complete understanding of the discussion as it develops. On the other hand, particularly if the road conditions are difficult, our analysis may be at a very superficial level. We may do little more than register that the discussion is between a man and a woman and is being conducted in English.

Let us now look at the stages of memorisation in more detail. Sensory stimulation reaching the individual from the environment via his sense receptors persists for only a brief time; none the less we are able to hold this stimulation in storage long enough to be able to use it. A seven figure telephone number, for example, will take only a moment to read but, for most people, a single reading will be enough to ensure that the number can be held in storage somewhere in the nervous system at least long enough for the number to be dialled accurately. Often the number will be lost to us as soon as we have dialled it and should the number be required again we will need to look it up once more. However, it is possible to commit the telephone number to some longer-term form of storage from which we will be able to withdraw it at will for long into the future. This telephone example illustrates the three stages of memory: the sensory memory when, following the reading, the number persists long enough to go into the short-term memory where it can be held long enough to be used, and the long-term memory where the number may be stored for months or even years.

These three stages of memory should not be thought of as located in three discrete and independent stores within the brain; the three stages are too closely interrelated for that. It is misleading to imagine that there is a straightforward progression with information passing in one direction only from the sensory store to the short-term memory and then, on occasions, on to the long-term memory. The content of long-term memory does often come from short-term memory, but what is already in long-term memory may influence what is extracted from the sensory memory for closer attention in short-term memory and also influence the way material from short-term memory is organised for long-term storage. The three stages are, perhaps, better thought of as different operating characteristics of a single memory system. The three stages are merely descriptions of the way memory looks if its operation is analysed at different periods of time after an event — after a second or two, after 30 seconds to a minute and after an hour, a day or even years.

Sensory Memory

Clear evidence for a very short-term store of information in a sensory memory comes from the work of Sperling (1960). Using a tachisto-scope to control exposure time he displayed to his subjects an array of twelve letters arranged in three rows of four. The exposure time for the display was very brief, 50 milliseconds. Sperling asked his subjects to try to recall the letters they had seen in one of two different ways. In the whole report condition he asked his subjects to recall all the letters they had seen in the display immediately after the presentation. He found that on average his subjects could only recall about four letters. In the partial report condition subjects heard a tone immediately after the display had appeared which indicated which of the three rows was to be recalled. For example a high tone indicated the top row, a low tone the bottom row. Under this condition the subjects could accurately recall any row. Sperling concluded that all of the informa-tion in the display must have been available to the subjects immediately after the display had appeared, but that this information very quickly faded. The time that it took to recall four letters was long enough for the rest of the information to decay. We are not aware of the information that is in the sensory memory until we have processed it in some way and, as Sperling's experiment illustrates, we can be selective about what part of the display we will process before it disappears. Sperling controlled his subjects' selection with a tone: in real life situations it is often material in our long-term memory, which has come from our past experience, that controls what information we will process from the immediate sensory store before the information has decayed.

All our perceptual systems seem to have some way of maintaining the effects of stimulation in sensory storage for a brief moment after it has been experienced. The role of the sensory memory appears to be to hold information long enough for some of it to be transferred to short-term memory. Loss from sensory memory can be caused by decay with the passage of time or by the contents being masked by new incoming information. There is nothing that we can do to improve or extend the effectiveness of the sensory memory and it is not until the information that has been selected from it has passed to the short-term memory that its contents overtly influence our behaviour. Sensory memory is involved in adult learning but from the practical point of view it is of little significance.

Short-term or Working Memory

We all need to remember information that is of only short-lived significance to us. If we are driving a car we need to remember where we are going, if we are buying a drink in the bar we need to remember how much money we tendered in order to check whether our change is correct. There would be little point in being able to recall such information days or even hours later but at the time it is essential that the information in our memory is accurate. This kind of information, that we do not need to keep but which is essential for the details of our daily lives, is held in the short-term or, as it is sometimes called, working memory. There are very real limits to the capacity of this working memory and it is very easily overloaded.

We are all aware of the fact that we can only take in a limited amount of new information at once. Miller (1956) has shown that for most subjects six or seven digits is the maximum that can be held in store at any one time. This can easily be demonstrated by dictating several strings of digits of various lengths to a subject and asking him to recall them immediately. As soon as the string goes over seven digits the majority of subjects will fail to recall them all unless they can find some way of coding some of the digits in ways that are already familiar. For example, with a new telephone number we may recognise the first few digits as representing an exchange and, because they are already well established in our long-term memory, find we can treat them as though they were one unit. This illustration demonstrates how coding material in short-term memory, by drawing on information in long-term memory, can extend the effective capacity of short-term memory.

The information in short-term memory is very vulnerable to loss through the reception of new information from the sensory memory. Because its capacity is strictly limited something must be displaced if we try to put more information into short-term memory than it can hold. If someone asks us to tell them the time as we go over to the telephone to dial the seven digit number that we have just looked up, the telephone number will be lost. Another example of overloading may occur if distracting thoughts enter short-term memory from our long-term memory. Information is lost from short-term memory almost as soon as it goes in unless some effort is made to rehearse it. In the case of the telephone number we need to repeat it over and over to ourselves. Information will persist in short-term memory for as long as we pay attention to it.

Information goes into short-term memory almost instantaneously; rehearsal may be necessary to keep it there but its initial reception is effortless. The other interesting characteristic of short-term memory is that the information that it contains is immediately available for use. The short-term memory, then, is very much the working memory. The perceptions of the moment and the thoughts that come from the past are both brought together, worked upon and made use of here. Its shortcoming is that its capacity is very limited and its persistence very brief.

Long-term Memory

Long-term memory, on the other hand, seems to have unlimited capacity and in many instances an indefinite duration. No one has yet had to curtail their learning because their long-term memory was full; old people can readily recall material learned in childhood after a lifetime of subsequent learning and experience. Sometimes we are surprised by what information we do hold in our long-term memory. Some trivial stimulus jogs the memory and we find we can recall scenes and events that we might well have thought long forgotten.

Most of the time we are unaware of just how great the capacity and persistence of our long-term memory can be. Under hypnosis or in psychotherapy people sometimes find that they can recall, with great accuracy, the detailed happenings of the past. The problem we often have with long-term memory is to get out the information that we have stored there. The ease, or otherwise, with which we can recall information from long-term memory seems to depend upon how the information we seek is organised, upon the extent to which it is integrated with other things that we know. We will explore further the importance of the organisation of ideas as a contribution to effective learning in subsequent chapters.

Although the capacity of the long-term memory is effectively limitless, there is a very real limit to the rate at which new information can be entered into long-term storage. Short-term memory, as we have seen, is limited to holding about seven items of information at any one time. The rate of entry of new information into long-term memory is limited to about one item of new information every four or five seconds. An unfamiliar seven digit telephone number will take about thirty seconds to get into long-term memory. In other words it will need to be rehearsed in short-term memory for thirty seconds before it is learned (Simon, 1969). Between them the limitations on the capacity of short-term memory and the rate of entry to long-term memory set the limits for adult learning.

Analysis, Organisation and Recall

The story does not end here, for we do have ways of overcoming some of the limitations of these capacities. We must now begin to consider the significance of the level of analysis of the information which is to be learned. We noted earlier that although a telephone number may have seven digits, if the first few digits represent a familiar exchange, then these digits will be coded as just one item of information. The limitations on our memory can often be overcome by the brain analysing the information and coding it to make smaller units before it goes forward for storage in the long-term memory.

A small child learning to spell will hold individual letters in the short-term memory and will commit one letter to long-term storage every five seconds or so; the adolescent learning foreign vocabulary will hold individual words in short-term memory and attempt to get a new word of many letters into long-term memory every five seconds. An experienced adult, reading at a rate well in excess of two hundred words a minute, will hold the *meaning* of a passage in his short-term memory rather than the individual words and will commit the gist of the passage to long-term memory.

The size of the units of information that can be dealt with in short- and long-term memory is dependent on the existing knowledge of the learner. The more the learner's past experience can be drawn upon to enable him to analyse and organise new information into familiar patterns, the easier it will be to commit the new material to memory. If a mass of new information can be seen as yet another illustration of a well understood principle then it will be more readily accommodated in both short- and long-term memory than if all the detail had to be retained.

The level at which new information is analysed and organised is also the key to its subsequent recall from long-term memory. The more effectively new information can be integrated with what is already known, the easier it is to recall it. New information that has no meaning for the learner in terms of the familiar must be learned in its entirety. Likewise it will need to be recalled in its entirety, there will be no cues from the familiar to help in its reconstruction. We will have more to say about the importance of the analysis and organisation of information for adult learning in later chapters.

Some Influences on Adult Learning

The mechanisms of memory that we have been considering operate for all human learners whether they are in the juvenile or adult phase of their life. Some of the other ideas which we will consider in later chapters are equally applicable to old and young alike. There are, however, a number of special factors that can influence the learning of adults. We will consider them in greater detail in later chapters, but it may be useful to be alerted to them now.

Adults tend to underestimate their ability to learn new material by giving too much emphasis to their school experience whilst over-looking the value of their more recent extensive informal learning experiences. Adults in their forties and fifties have about the same ability to learn as they had in their twenties and thirties but age, none the less, does have an influence upon them. The older learner will learn to his maximum capacity only if the teaching programme is suitable. The short-term memory capacity hardly declines at all with age, but unfortunately it does become much more liable to breakdown through the effects of overloading as adults move into their forties and fifties. A very slight interruption or distraction to attention while information is being received will cause the older learner to forget immediately. As a result older learners experience some difficulties with tasks that are paced, stressful or require the interpretation of complex instructions.

The previous educational experience of the adult can have a great influence on the effectiveness of his learning. The greater the adult's formal educational level the better he is likely to cope with most learning tasks in adulthood. This effect is almost certainly due to a number of factors including the nature of the learner's already existing intellectual framework. The better educated the learner the more likely the new learning can be integrated into existing knowledge. The older learner has greater problems when he tries to learn something new than when he advances his knowledge in a field that is already familiar.

Education and socio-economic background are factors that influence an adult's attitude and motivation towards new learning, particularly if the learning is to take place in a formal setting. An adult who has had successful educational experiences in childhood is likely to approach a new learning experience with a positive attitude both towards the instruction and his own performance as a learner. He is likely to be fairly strongly motivated to achieve. An adult who has had a poor school record will probably see any formal learning situation as yet another opportunity to fail and avoid it if at all possible. If forced to undergo formal instruction he may well experience a high level of stress which will impair his learning performance.

The way an individual perceives himself will have an important influence on how he approaches new learning experiences. The origins of self-perception lie in our interpretations of other people's perceptions of us. Those who teach adults can often have a significant influence when it comes to convincing a reluctant learner that he can cope with a learning task that he considers beyond his capacity.

There are many different ways in which the social setting for formal adult learning can be organised. Different contexts for learning such as lectures, seminars, tutorials, practical work, independent learning and so on seem to suit some subject matter and some learners better than others. We will review some of the evidence on this.

Adult learning is influenced by many different factors; in our attempt to understand it better we will concentrate on some of these factors one by one. We will be rather like an explorer in a forest at night with a flash light; he can only direct it at one tree at a time yet he is attempting to get an impression of the whole forest. Adult learning is complex, the ideas in this book as a whole, it is hoped, will build up to give an indication of its complexity.

2 ADULT LEARNING: A THEORETICAL OVERVIEW

Theoretical Approaches to Learning

Introduction

Psychologists have been theorising and carrying out research on learning since psychology became an experimental science during the closing decades of the nineteenth century. Although many of the psychologists who have investigated human learning have held some common assumptions about the way in which the learning process should be conceptualised, the variations and discrepancies between the approaches of different schools of psychology are often very great. At the present stage in the development of psychology it is not possible to provide a comprehensive and closely integrated theoretical account of how human adult learning comes about.

In this chapter an attempt will be made to outline some of the major theoretical contributions to the study of human learning. In the following four chapters many of the ideas that emerge here will be considered in more detail as they relate to the learning of information, strategies, skills and social behaviour. The emphasis throughout will be upon approaches that have applications to the problems of learning in adult life. Much of what will be said about learning will have implications for and applications to the work of educators. As we have already noted, however, much adult learning takes place in an informal way outside educational and training establishments as a process incidental to everyday living. Usually this incidental learning is advantageous to the individual but, it is worth noting, some forms of incidental adult learning, such as the acquisition of excessive responses of fear and anxiety in everyday situations, can lead to considerable distress. Some of the approaches outlined here relate to these forms of incidental learning too. In different ways the theoretical work described here has applications to a broad sample of the numerous forms and aspects of learning that are likely to be encountered in everyday adult life.

We have defined learning as a relatively permanent change in our potential for performance as the result of our past interaction with the environment. Let us examine this definition a little more closely. There are some changes in the potential for performance that are the result of maturation or ageing. The young child acquires the potential to stand upright or to use language as the result of biological maturation. The old person's strength of grip may weaken as the result of ageing. These changes do not depend on the nature of the individual's interaction with the environment and so are excluded from our definition of learning. Other changes in our potential for performance may come about as the result of illness or the application of drugs. Happily such changes are normally short-lived and would not fit into our definition of learning either. Although what has been learned may often stay with us for many years, we do forget and hence the change in our potential for performance is best defined as only relatively permanent.

Psychologists working within the behaviourist tradition, who regard observable behaviour as the sole permissible data for the science of psychology have argued that learning should be defined in operational terms, in terms of observable changes in behaviour. For an experimental psychologist, an operational approach to defining learning does have much to commend it. In practice it is not usually possible to find objective and reliable confirmation for learning without relying on some form of behavioural evidence. In research on learning in sub-human species changes in overt behaviour are usually the only objective evidence for learning that the experimenter can use. Although human subjects may tell us that they have learned a new skill from watching, for example, a television programme, until we have seen them carry out the skill, we cannot be certain that their verbal report is accurate. None the less, it is quite possible that learning may take place in an individual in the absence of any immediately observable change in behaviour. One may learn from reading a book how to replace a tap washer. There has been a change in one's potential for performance but it may only be years later when faced with a leaky tap that this potential manifests itself as overt behaviour. Our definition may be too loose for the strict behavioural psychologist but for a consideration of adult learning it does seem a more realistic one.

Let us now move on to consider some of the major theoretical approaches to the study of learning. During the first half of this century two very different ways of thinking about learning developed: that of the stimulus-response associationists, and that of the Gestalt psychologists. The stimulus-response associationists were concerned with identifying the successive steps in learning whilst the psychologists working within the Gestalt tradition took the view that successful learning resulted from the learner integrating and organising what was perceived or studied.

Trial and Error Learning

The first associationist, E.L. Thorndike (1874-1949) attempted to investigate how it was that specific responses became linked with specific stimuli. He conducted experiments with animals over a number of years and came to the conclusion that the development of bonds or connections between stimulus and response came about as the result of a process of trial and error. In a typical Thorndike trial and error learning experiment a hungry cat was imprisoned in a specially constructed cage or puzzle box. A dish of food was placed outside the cage and beyond the reach of the cat. The cat could escape from the box only if it succeeded in operating a specially constructed system of latches. The novice cat placed in the puzzle box for the first time clawed at the bars of the box and made many random movements that contributed nothing to its escape before, by chance, it succeeded in operating the latches and escaping to enjoy the food. Over a number of trials Thorndike found there was a gradual, though somewhat erratic, decrease in errors until a time was eventually reached when the cat placed in the box would effect its escape immediately. As the result of his experiments Thorndike formulated his Law of Effect (1898) which states that acts followed by a state of affairs which the individual does not avoid and which he often tries to preserve or attain, are selected or fixated. Thorndike believed that the new association forged between the stimulus and the response was reflected in a biological change in the nervous system; it has never been possible to demonstrate this experimentally. The Law of Effect stresses the importance of a learner's efforts being followed by success. Although the details of Thorndike's experimental work are of little obvious relevance to the learning of adults, a great deal of human learning can be accounted for in terms of the Law of Effect. Many of Thornkdike's ideas have been carried much further in the work of B.F. Skinner with operant conditioning. Thorndike's trial and error learning was a form of operant conditioning and we will examine this influential approach to learning in this chapter. Thorndike's most significant contribution was his formulation of the Law of Effect.

Classical Conditioning

Whilst the cat in Thorndike's trial and error learning experiments was active in trying to escape and learned as a direct consequence of its own activity, there is another sort of learning which has been analysed in stimulus-response terms that can come about even though the learner is passive — it is called classical conditioning. It was a Russian physiologist, Ivan Pavlov (1849-1936), who did the pioneering work in the study of classical conditioning. In his basic experimental procedure Pavlov showed that the sound of a bell could cause a dog to salivate if on a number of previous occasions the bell had been rung as the dog was fed. Through simultaneous presentation an association, which had not previously existed, had been built up between a stimulus (the sound of the bell) and a response (salivation). Learning had occurred. The dogs had learned, or been conditioned, to respond to a previously neutral stimulus. Before going on to consider some of the implications of these celebrated experiments for adult learning, it will be helpful to identify some of the basic terms used in connection with classical conditioning.

The conditioned stimulus is the stimulus which is neutral at the start but which acquires the power to produce a response as a result of the conditioning procedure. In the above example the sound of the bell is the conditioned stimulus. The unconditioned stimulus is a stimulus which produces the specific response involved in the procedure before the conditioning takes place. In the above experiment it is the food that is the unconditioned stimulus, since it consistently causes the dog to salivate. The unconditioned response is the response that naturally occurs before the conditioning procedure takes place. In our experiment it is the salivation, contraction of the stomach muscles, and so on that follow directly upon the presentation of the food to the dog. Any responses that are mediated by the autonomic nervous system can be involved in classical conditioning. The autonomic nervous system controls, amongst other things, responses connected with emotional behaviour, such as changes in heart rate, respiration, blood pressure, stomach activity and the electrical resistance of the skin. The conditioned response is the name given to the response to the previously neutral stimulus which is learned as a result of the conditioning procedure. Whilst the conditioned response is often very similar to the unconditioned response it is never exactly the same. In our experiment the conditioned response would involve less secretion of saliva than the unconditioned response. For this reason it is important to distinguish the conditioned response from the unconditioned response.

Pavlov found that once a response had been conditioned then it would be produced by other stimuli similar to the conditioned stimulus. He called this phenomenon stimulus generalisation. In our experiment once the conditioning to the bell has taken place, the ringing of another bell with a different tone to the original will also produce a response of salivation. The closer the new stimulus is to the original conditioned stimulus, the greater is the level of conditioned response.

Although classical conditioning is a very simple type of learning it can have very far reaching effects on human behaviour, for it is the mechanism through which many of our responses of pleasure or fear and anxiety are acquired. It is the kind of learning that underlies the acquisition of the emotional component of our attitudes.

Consider the long-term effects on a person's life that the following episode might have, perhaps affecting his choice of subject specialisation at school, his career options and, at a later date, his attitudes to his children's learning. A schoolboy has been working on a maths problem; unfortunately he makes a careless slip in his calculations and his answer is incorrect. The teacher, who is in a bad mood following a late night and a row with his wife over breakfast, comes round to look at the work, spots the careless mistake and, instead of giving a gentle admonition, pillories the boy at great length in front of his classmates. The boy is made very embarrassed and anxious. At long last the teacher lets him off the hook and the lesson comes to an end. If any classical conditioning has taken place during this episode, and it would be more likely if the boy is an introvert by temperament, much of the anxiety and embarrassment the teacher created will be reactivated the next time the boy comes to tackle a maths problem.

The first maths problem is a conditioned stimulus; it is neutral to begin with but, as the result of the conditioning procedure, it becomes associated with the teacher's criticism. The teacher's criticism is the unconditioned stimulus which, in any but the most recalcitrant schoolboy, would produce the unconditioned response of anxiety and embarrassment. As a consequence of stimulus generalisation the next maths problem, which is sufficiently like the first, reactivates the associations learned between the first maths problem and the teacher's criticism. If the boy is sufficiently disturbed then he may generalise his reaction onto all his school experiences.

If the teacher is aware of the dangers of some classical conditioning having occurred in this situation, then he may well attempt to put right the trouble his bad tempered behaviour has caused. If a conditioned stimulus (in this case the maths problem) is presented on a number of occasions unaccompanied by the unconditioned stimulus (the teacher's ill humour), then the conditioned response (the boy's learned anxiety) will gradually fade away and eventually cease altogether. The conditioned response has been extinguished, to use the language of classical conditioning. However, even when the conditioned response has been extinguished, the teacher still cannot be confident that the damage is repaired, for there is frequently a spontaneous recovery of conditioned responses after they have been extinguished. This clearly establishes that, although a response may be extinguished, it is not necessarily forgotten or lost. The boy's anxiety about maths may well revive after a week or two, but at a lower level of intensity, as the result of spontaneous recovery. If the teacher then does anything to reinforce the conditioned response, such as criticising the boy again, or, bearing the influence of stimulus generalisation in mind, criticises another student in a similar fashion, then the conditioned response may become very strongly established. If nothing is done to reinforce the spontaneously recovered response, it will extinguish again. There may be several more episodes of spontaneous recovery before the response dies away completely, but each recovery is likely to see the conditioned response at a lower level of intensity.

The example of the schoolboy acquiring an emotional response to maths has been explored at length. If the boy's initial conditioned response is reinforced on numerous occasions then he may become alienated from any learning experiences that involve mathematics for the rest of his life. It is possible to think of many examples of the application of classical conditioning to adult learning. Many specific fear responses associated with hospitals and dentists can be seen as the direct consequence of classical conditioning. Many mothers have given up breast feeding their babies because of the unsympathetic comments of a nurse or the dissatisfied bawling of their infant, many sportsmen have finished with their sport following a bad accident and equally, many people have studied a subject at evening classes because they enjoyed the warm, friendly atmosphere the tutor created, or read a book or seen a play because they enjoyed the author's previous one. All of these forms of behaviour, and many more involving emotional responses, will have been influenced, at least in part, by classical conditioning. In spite of the impact on our emotional and attitudinal learning, classical conditioning is very limited in its scope. First, it is only applicable to situations in which the individual is passive. Pavlov's dog stood passively in a harness whilst it was classically conditioned to salivate to the sound of the bell; our schoolboy could do nothing to prevent himself being classically conditioned in the situation his schoolmaster created. Secondly, it is only responses controlled by the autonomic nervous sytem, the visceral components of our responses of fear, anger, anxiety, pleasure or sense of well-being, that can be classically conditioned. Teachers classically condition their students, whether they intend to or not, by the emotional climate they create in the learning environment.

Operant Conditioning

Still in the stimulus-response tradition, B.F. Skinner (1904 —) has voluntary behaviour at the heart of operant (or instrumental) conditioning. If the subject does not emit a response of his own accord with operant conditioning, no learning can occur. Skinner's work has many more obvious applications to our day to day learning than does classical conditioning. Indeed, some extreme advocates of operant conditioning would argue that almost all human learning can be interpreted in its terms (Skinner, 1971).

Skinner carried out most of his basic research on rats and pigeons. These are species that enable the experimenter to exert the maximum control over many of the variables that may affect learning. For example, Skinner sometimes expresses the level of motivation of an animal as a percentage loss of body weight, and genetic variables can be almost eliminated with animals that can be bred rapidly with only small genetic variation. However, much of Skinner's basic research has been confirmed with human subjects (Ackerman, 1972), and there are many confirmations of the validity of his ideas from everyday experience.

Skinner is an extreme behaviourist; he has no time for theoretical abstractions invented in an attempt to account for the working of behaviour (Skinner, 1972). Knowledge of physiology will not alter the behavioural facts. His prime concern is to be able to predict behaviour accurately and ultimately to be in a position to modify it. He believes that descriptions of behaviour, and relations between behaviour and variables which we can be certain of, are reliable and sufficient in themselves. No other explanations are necessary.

Operant conditioning has to do with the effects of reward and punishment. The fundamental principle of operant conditioning is that behaviour is governed by its consequences. We do not behave in a random fashion but in order to bring about certain desirable objectives. Through experience we come to learn that these objectives are more likely to be reached if we behave in one way rather than another. Consequences that increase the frequency of our behaving in one way rather than another are referred to as reinforcers. Goals, rewards and incentives are all examples of positive reinforcers; achieving the goal or obtaining the reward or incentive brings about positive reinforcement. Escaping from unpleasant or dangerous consequences are examples of negative reinforcement. Reinforcement always results in some improvement for the learner. With positive reinforcement something desirable happens, for example, the machinist sews a straight seam or the darts player scores a bull's-eye. In the case of negative reinforcement something unpleasant ceases or is reduced in potency; when the driver brakes slowly the car skids less on the black ice. Reinforcement leads to learning through the Law of Effect.

Punishment can also influence behaviour. When punishment follows as a consequence of a response, it leads to a decrease in the probability of the response being repeated. Punishment can be distinguished from negative reinforcement because it marks a moment for the learner when things get worse, either because positive reinforcers are lost, as is the case with fines in everday life, or because an unpleasant state of affairs such as physical pain or social rejection follows.

Positive Reinforcement

The three outcomes of behaviour which bring about learning, positive reinforcement, negative reinforcement and punishment, are central to operant conditioning; the linchpin of the process is positive reinforcement. The following study illustrates the way positive reinforcement can be used to improve the behaviour of patients in a chronic psychiatric ward (Ayllon and Azrin, 1968). In the typical psychiatric ward a patient is more likely to obtain the attention that he seeks from the overworked nursing staff if he behaves in a maladaptive way, such as refusing to feed himself, talking incoherently or acting aggressively towards other patients. When he sits reading quietly, feeds himself or engages another patient in friendly conversation the nursing staff will pay him scant attention. The operant conditioning model would predict that the longer the patient stays in the ward where he gets positive reinforcement for anti-social behaviour the more his behaviour will deteriorate. Ayllon and his team arranged instead that positive reinforcers in the form of special tokens that could be exchanged for rewards such as cigarettes, food and social attention were given whenever a patient engaged in certain forms of desirable behaviour, such as making his bed, dressing and feeding himself. The study demonstrated that a token economy of this kind can lead to a marked improvement in the behaviour of even severely disturbed psychiatric patients.

Our experiences in everyday life are rich with instances of the power of positive reinforcement. We work for money or the pleasure that comes from doing a job well; we take care with our appearance because it gains us social approval; we write or paint because of the satisfaction that comes from creating something new. In many instances the positive reinforcement that comes as the result of our behaviour ensures that we continue with this behaviour in the future.

Shaping

When someone is attempting to control the behaviour of another, using operant conditioning techniques, it is sometimes necessary to use a shaping procedure to bring about the desired response. Shaping involves reinforcing a series of successive approximations of the behaviour that it is intended should be learned. When the behaviour which is desired is slow to appear, responses that resemble the response at least in part are positively reinforced. Gradually the criterion for the reinforcement is shifted from the approximation towards the desired response. Suppose that a tennis coach intends to improve a player's backhand stroke. At first the coach would express approval (positive reinforcement) for a crude and clumsy version of the desired stroke, but as the positive reinforcement increases the frequency with which the player produces this crude stroke, the coach becomes more demanding in the quality of the stroke required to merit his approval. Of course the coach will also demonstrate the correct stroke and give the player other guidance, but this shaping using positive reinforcement is crucial to establishing the new stroke.

In the case of the tennis coach giving social approval for a well played stroke the reinforcement is extrinsic to the task. Operant conditioning also functions where the reinforcement is intrinsic to the task. For example, the tennis player may steadily improve his strokes through practice against a wall without the helpful comments and social reinforcement provided by the coach. In this case the player obtains feedback from his performance as he watches the effects of his stroke patterns upon the flight of the ball. A good, accurate stroke will be reinforced by the player noting that the ball has behaved as he intended it should. As we shall see in Chapter 5, when an adult is learning a skill, it is important that he learns to use the intrinsic feedback that comes from the performance of the skill itself rather than relying on the assessment of his performance made by a teacher or instructor. One interesting implication of the reinforcing power of intrinsic feedback is that it is possible for a learner to train himself once he can evaluate the feedback; training does not necessarily require a teacher. The teacher's special contribution is to ensure that the learner makes the most effective use of intrinsic feedback and to provide extrinsic feedback until that stage has been reached.

Schedules of Reinforcement

In some operant conditioning situations the learner receives reinforcement every time he makes an appropriate response. Each time the driver turns the steering wheel on a moving car, the vehicle moves in the appropriate direction. Skinner would describe the learner as being on a continuous schedule of reinforcement. In the initial stage of learning a new form of behaviour a continuous schedule of reinforcement is necessary. Once they are established some forms of behaviour may be reinforced only after the passage of a fixed interval of time; the weekly wage earner receives reinforcement for his working behaviour when his employer pays him at the end of the week, the student receives feedback and reinforcement from his teacher when the weekly assignment is handed back marked. Skinner has investigated the effect of different patterns, or schedules, of reinforcement on learning.

Working with animal subjects Skinner found that a fixed-interval schedule in which the animal was reinforced, say, once every five minutes, results in a slow response for a while after the reinforcement has been given but as the end of the interval approaches there is a speeding up of the rate of response. In a fixed ratio schedule, where the animal is reinforced after making a set number of responses, say once every tenth response, the animal works considerably faster than with a continuous schedule of reinforcement. A human parallel would be with a worker who was paid as soon as a certain amount of work had been done.

Frequently the schedules of reinforcement for human behaviour have unpredictable characteristics. A variable interval schedule is one in which the learner is reinforced after intervals of time that vary in an unpredictable way. Variable interval schedules produce a steady rate of response. Typical examples from everyday situations include the fisherman, who never knows when a fish may bite, or the schedule of the radar operator who never knows when an image may appear on the screen. In some situations it is the ratio of responses which change in an unpredictable fashion. In a variable ratio schedule it is the number of responses that may be reinforced that is unpredictable. The man at the fruit machine never knows whether the next pull on the handle may not result in a cascade of coins, the novice playwright can never be sure his next play will not be a winner. A very high rate of response can result from the use of this schedule.

In Skinner's terms behaviour is contingent upon reinforcement; when reinforcement is no longer available then the behaviour will extinguish completely or decrease until it is no more frequent than it was before the conditioning took place. Other things being equal, the amount of response before extinction is complete is related to the number of reinforcements received during the conditioning phase. The more reinforcement is given, the longer the responses persist. The schedule of reinforcement that was in operation when the reinforcement came to an end has a significant influence on the speed with which extinction comes about. Behaviour reinforced on a continuous schedule extinguishes most rapidly. The individual who is accustomed to his radio playing every time he turns it on soon puts the radio aside when he turns it on and nothing happens. A partial reinforcement schedule extinguishes more slowly. A variable interval or ratio schedule of reinforcement will produce a long period of stable response before the response extinguishes or reverts to the pre-conditioning level. The fisherman will keep casting for hours even though no fish bites; the inveterate gambler will keep risking his stake money although none of his bets succeeds.

Just as with classical conditioning, extinguished responses may spontaneously recur from time to time. Even though the psychiatric patients had their maladaptive behaviour extinguished and replaced with more socially acceptable forms, the patients still reverted occasionally to their old ways. If a spontaneously recovered response is reinforced again the extinguished behaviour will soon revert to the former level.

Negative Reinforcement and Punishment

Let us now look briefly at negative reinforcement and then punishment. Negative reinforcement is at work when conditioning becomes contingent upon the removal or termination of some unpleasant stimulus. For example, some students work excessively hard not in order to achieve the positive reinforcement of academic success but to avoid the humiliation of failure. Negative reinforcement is also at work in escape learning. This occurs when the learner behaves in a particular way in order to avoid unpleasant consequences. We might well put off visiting the dentist if we know that some painful dental work will be carried out on our teeth. Many people offered the chance to retrain for a new job following a redundancy will stay unemployed to escape the blow to their self-esteem they fear a poor performance on a training scheme would bring. With negative reinforcement it is the action that leads to something unpleasant being prevented that is learned.

In some cases unpleasant consequences are threatened in order to force a subject to behave in a particular way. This variety of negative reinforcement is referred to as aversive control and it is used quite frequently in social life. Acceptable social behaviour is often maintained by the threat of legal or other punishment. In the family the adolescent is threatened with early bed unless his behaviour improves or the wife is faced with the husband's bad temper unless she complies with his wishes; at work the employee arrives on time to avoid losing an hour's pay: all these are examples of the use of aversive control. It can be a very effective method of altering behaviour, but it has the weakness that the learners (or victims) often feel that they have been manipulated or coerced. The victim may use escape procedures which would then be negatively reinforced. The adolescent may leave home, the wife seek a divorce and the employee change his job.

In the case of punishment an unpleasant stimulus is contingent upon the subject's response being made. Punishment leads to a decrease in the probability of the response being made. Punishment is very widely used in everyday life. Speeding is fined, poor academic performance is given low marks, social deviants are rejected by the group. Punishment is a very effective way of controlling behaviour — but only in the short term. If a parent shouts at a child who is misbehaving the bad behaviour is likely to stop at once, at least for a while. Of course, the rapid improvement in behaviour that punishment can achieve acts as positive reinforcement for the punisher. The parent who is provoked into using punishment often feels a high level of aggression and hostility towards the child, administering the punishment may give a chance for these pent up emotions to be vented which can also act as positive reinforcement for the punisher.

In spite of its attractions for the punisher, punishment is not a very effective form of behaviour control. Although the unwanted behaviour may be suppressed for the moment, the learner gets no reinforcement of more desirable alternative forms of behaviour. This perhaps accounts for the high rate of recidivism among criminals. The punishment society metes out offers no opportunity for other more desirable forms of behaviour to be established. As soon as the immediate threat of punishment is removed, the criminal often returns to his old patterns of well-reinforced behaviour.

Another short-coming of punishment is that it is often accompanied by emotional responses on the part of the learner which through the process of classical conditioning can produce long-term anxiety and disturbance. We saw earlier the possible long-term effects of an excessively punitive teacher on a student's attitudes towards mathematics. Many adults hesitate to attempt any form of formal learning because of the negative feelings towards teachers and educational institutions aroused as the result of earlier traumatic experiences in school.

When punishment is necessary, it should be used with care. It is probably most appropriately used as a way to inhibit undesirable responses so that an opportunity can be found to positively reinforce more acceptable forms of behaviour.

The operant conditioning model is probably the most significant single contribution to the study of learning. As can be seen from the illustrative examples given in this chapter, the model can be used to account for numerous examples of the acquisition and maintenance of new forms of behaviour in everyday life. No one concerned with the mechanisms of adult learning can afford to be unaware of the details of Skinner's contribution to the study of learning. Many of the recent developments in educational technology can trace their antecedents back to Skinner's extremely influential work with linear programmed learning. With the typical linear programme, the presentation of the material is so arranged that the learner will make nothing but correct responses throughout the course of the instruction and, as a consequence, receive nothing but positive reinforcement. Admittedly this approach avoids the detrimental side effects of the punishment associated with errors, but most recent developments regard this exclusive insistence on positive reinforcement as unnecessarily constricting. Effective adult learning is not restricted to the acquisition of simple statements that can be recognised as right or wrong, but involves the integration of new material into a complex network of already existing ideas and experiences.

The Gestalt Approach to Learning

We will now move from the stimulus-response associationist tradition to consider the contribution to the study of learning of the Gestalt school of psychologists. Gestalt is a German word which means form, figure, shape or pattern and this group of psychologists, which included W. Köhler (1887-1967), F. Koffka (1886-1941), M. Wertheimer (1886-1943) and K. Lewin (1890-1947), acquired their title because they emphasised the organisation of perception into 'good form' and 'good pattern'. Early work on perception had been mainly concerned with threshold levels: for example, what increase in illumination was necessary to produce a just noticeable difference in brightness? In 1912 Max Wertheimer argued that perception could not be understood through a study of the component parts. The perceiver or the learner attempts to organise and integrate what he perceives or studies in order to achieve an overall pattern or 'Gestalt'. Wertheimer believed it was futile to attempt to analyse the whole into discrete elements or parts as the stimulus-response psychologists in particular attempted to do.

The prime interest of the Gestalt school was in the area of perception. Wertheimer formulated four laws of perception which together contribute to the general principle of *Prägnanz* or meaningfulness. This principle states that a subject will structure the perceptual field in as simple and clear a way as possible in order to impose meaning on it. The four laws of similarity, proximity, closure and good continuation account for the way a subject structures his perceptual field. Similarity, for example, states that in a visual field we tend to pick out and group together as a unit those parts that are similar; proximity, that items close together tend to become integrated as a complete and separate unit. Closure implies that where there are gaps in a visual presentation such as with incomplete outlines or pictures, the observer will tend to close the gaps in his perception of the material. Continuation describes the way, in our perception, we will carry forward straight lines or smooth curves even though the continuation has not been drawn in. The art of the cartoonist is dependent on the workings of the four laws. The Gestalt psychologists would have argued that no cartoon can be understood by analysing the individual strokes that make it up. The whole is greater than the sum of its parts. That extra element of meaningfulness that comes when we recognise five pencil strokes as the face of a well-known politician, for example, results from the four laws of perception. The same four laws apply to the perception of aural and other sensory input. They account for our perception of tune and harmony in music instead of merely a number of independent notes, according to the Gestalt school.

Insightful Learning

The Gestalt psychologists' initial interest was in the field of perception, but they recognised that the basic principles of perception were also applicable to learning, so they transferred their interest to this topic. Their best known experiments in this area were carried out by Köhler (1925) on animal problem solving. Working with chimpanzees, Köhler conducted a whole series of experiments which appeared to demonstrate that when faced with a problem such as how to obtain food that was out of reach, the chimpanzee did not tackle it in a trial and error fashion as Thorndike would have predicted, but came to a sudden, insightful solution which seemed to be the result of the animal restructuring the components of the problem, very much as with the cartoon, where the five lines are restructured to give the perception of a face.

Some of the characteristics of insightful learning follow. The solution of the problem comes suddenly. We have all experienced at some time or another the flash of inspiration that leads to the solution of a problem that has engaged us for some time. As soon as the solution is perceived the learner can immediately proceed to use the insight. The solution to the original problem can be transferred to similar problems in a different setting. Once we have had the insight that the top half of the radiator is cold because there has been a build-up of air, we can put the problem right immediately by bleeding the radiator and can transfer this answer to many other similar contexts.

Max Wertheimer showed that identical processes of insightful learning to those described by Köhler occurred with children's learning (Wertheimer, 1961). For a time it appeared that the Gestalt school had identified a different kind of learning altogether from that described by Thorndike and subsequent workers in the stimulus-response tradition, such as Skinner. However, psychologists have since shown that insightful learning is in fact dependent on past experience. H.G. Birch (1945) showed that the apparently sudden solution to a problem is only likely to occur when the learner has had an opportunity to become familiar with the main features of the problem situation on earlier occasions. H.F. Harlow (1949) showed that insightful learning appeared to be dependent on previous trial and error learning. Harlow found that when both monkeys and young children were faced with a series of discrimination problems they made a natural progression from random trial and error learning to the apparently insightful learning studied by the Gestalt school. Both the monkeys and the children seemed to acquire strategies, or 'learning sets' as Harlow calls them, for solving the particular kinds of problems. They had 'learned how to learn' with this particular kind of problem. A great deal of adult learning seems to take the form of the insightful solution of problems. It is important to recognise that those sudden flashes of inspiration that enable us to get the car started on a wet morning or to find a new application for a familiar industrial technique are the result of previous experience and learning. Human learning seems to be hierarchical; our more impressive achievements involving cognitive learning such as the solving of complex problems, have as a prerequisite the mastery of simpler kinds of learning. This simpler learning seems best described in stimulus-response terms.

Gagné's Hierarchical Model of Learning

R.M. Gagné offers a very useful hierarchical model of learning which helps to clarify how the different forms of learning we have discussed so far may relate to each other. Gagné (1977) suggests that there are eight major types of mental processing. He calls the eight, signal learning, S-R learning, motor and verbal chain learning, multiple discrimination, concept learning, rule learning and problem solving. With the exception of signal learning these are arranged in a hierarchical fashion; learning at each level depends upon successful learning having already taken place at each of the preceding levels.

For successful learning to take place at any level in the hierarchy certain conditions must be met. Gagné distinguishes between conditions that are internal to the learner and those that are external to the learner. The internal conditions include what the learner must already be able to do before the new level of learning can take place; typically this means ensuring that the lower levels of learning have been mastered. The external conditions are typical of the kind that could be manipulated by a teacher, for example, the length of the practice, the nature of the feedback available to the learner and the incidence of reinforcement. Let us now review Gagné's eight types of learning.

Signal learning can be equated with Pavlov's classical conditioning. A conditioned stimulus (the signal) must be followed almost immediately by an unconditioned stimulus which produces an unconditioned reflexive, emotional response. After the combination of conditioned stimulus and unconditioned stimulus have occurred on a number of occasions, the conditioned stimulus (the signal) alone will precipitate the emotional response. As we have already seen, this kind of learning has a pervasive influence on the emotional and attitudinal learning of adults. Signal learning can occur in parallel with other learning at any level of Gagné's hierarchy.

Stimulus-response learning is at the lowest level in the hierarchy. For stimulus-response learning to occur there must be a voluntary response that the learner is capable of making and a stimulus to which he will react. The terminal response that the learner makes must be followed by some form of reinforcement; shaping procedures can be used in helping the learner acquire the precise response required. This is a basic form of operant conditioning.

Motor and verbal chain learning both come next, at the same level of the hierarchy; they differ in the nature of the material that is learned. With motor chaining, muscular responses that have already been learned as stimulus-response connections are performed one after another to produce a smooth sequence of physical movements. Whatever the length of the chain, the response to the initial stimulus acts as the stimulus for the next response and so on. The development of the chain depends on kinaesthetic feedback from the muscles, working in such a way that a response made at one place in the chain acts as a cue for the next link in the chain to be produced. Typical motor chains occur in writing your address on an envelope, parrying a thrust in fencing, setting up a milling machine or riding a surf board. When learning new motor chains the most important condition is for the learner to carry out the sequence of previously learned stimulus-response links in the correct order. The links need to be carried out in quick succession if the chain is to be established as a smooth sequence. Learning can occur in one trial but normally practice is required, particularly if it is a long or complex chain that is to be mastered. The final link in the chain, as with any successful operant conditioning, must result in the learner obtaining some form of reinforcement.

Verbal chain learning, or verbal association, may range from the learning of a couple of words or short phrases to memorising the principal French irregular verbs or learning one's part in a play. Again, as with motor chaining, each link of the chain must have been previously learned as a stimulus-response unit, but this time it is not kinaesthetic feedback which helps to establish each response as the stimulus for succeeding responses, but mediating connections between each verbal unit and the next. For example, the meaning of the words the actor has just spoken often give him the cue for the words he must say next. These mediating connections can take the form of verbal, visual or auditory cues. Sometimes it is where he is standing in relationship to other actors or what another actor has just said that prompts a particular speech. For effective verbal chaining to take place Gagne suggests that the verbal units must be presented in the right sequence and closely in time to one another. Learning can occur in one session but normally practice must be provided. The final link in the chain must lead to some form of reinforcement. This could, for example, take the form of confirmation that the chain had been correctly performed.

With multiple discrimination learning we move into the area of intellectual skills. In most subjects in formal education and in innumerable everyday learning situations the adult has to learn to make discriminations between people, objects, events, representations and symbols that are in some respects similar. Gagné's next level in the learning hierarchy is concerned with the way we learn to make these multiple discriminations. Suppose we want to pick out from a bunch of keys the key to the front door, how do we learn to discriminate this key from among many others of similar pattern and appearance? Likewise, how does a doctor discriminate between diseases with similar symptoms or a biologist discriminate between different varieties of moth? To begin with the learner must have already mastered each chain in the set where the discriminations are to be made. Each of the keys on the bunch should be familiar, the doctor should know the symptoms of each disease, the biologist be able to recognise each of the moths. In order to learn to make the discrimination between one stimulus and the next, each of the members of the set should be presented one at a time but close to each other and the learner should be prompted to recall the chain of associations for each. The order of presentation is best varied over a number of practice sessions. If need be the differences between the members of the set may be exaggerated during the learning period to make each member of the set as distinctive as possible. As the learner masters the discriminations the exaggerated details should be faded out. Finally the learner needs to have feedback about his progress for the feedback can in itself act as reinforcement.

Concept learning comes at the next level of Gagné's hierarchy. One way in which we respond to collections of things is by learning how to distinguish them from one another through multiple discrimination learning. Another way is to learn how to put things that have some differences into a class; we then respond to the individual instances as we would to any member of the class. For example, although we may be able to make the multiple discriminations necessary to recognise one make of car from another, when we are crossing the road we merely look out for cars; all cars hold the same danger for the pedestrian no matter what the make or model. In the same way, when we are attempting to understand ideas about human learning it can be helpful to be able to consider all reinforcers as a class even though their nature may vary greatly. Concept learning makes it possible for an individual to respond to a number of slightly different things as a class. Most instances of adult learning involve the acquisition of many new concepts. Learning a new concept normally involves acquiring a word which comes to stand for the concept (e.g., 'force' in physics or 'capital' in economics), and then acquiring the sense or meaning of the concept from encounters with positive and negative instances of the concept. Once the concept has been acquired the learner will be able to recognise fresh instances and will probably be capable of giving a verbal definition of the concept. As the acquisition of concepts is such an important part of adult learning we will consider this topic more fully in Chapter 3.

The next level in Gagné's hierarchical description of learning is concerned with the acquisition of rules. The ability which we have to respond to an enormous variety of situations and to perform effectively, despite the almost infinite variety in the stimulation that may reach us, makes it clear that we must have a prodigious ability to organise information. The basis of this organisation in our intellectual processing, according to Gagné, lies in the rules that we have learned. The existence of a rule can be inferred when an individual responds to a class of stimulus situations with a class of performances. It is often possible to give a verbal description of the rules that govern an individual's behaviour but frequently we apply rules without being able to state them formally. For example, few English speakers would have trouble in pronouncing words with a long 'a', such as 'gate', 'shame' and 'pane' differently from words with a short 'a' such as 'hat', 'ham' and 'pan', but they may well not be capable of stating the rule that governs their pronunciation. Gagné is concerned with how we acquire competence in using rules rather than with the learning of their definition. Almost all formal adult learning involving cognitive material requires us to learn rules. The typical academic course involves the learning of a whole hierarchy of rules; the overall objectives of the course involve the most complex rules and their attainment is dependent upon the acquisition of simpler rules. These simpler rules in their turn require the learning of still simpler rules and these in their turn may be dependent upon previously learned concepts. Once a person has learned a rule he becomes capable of responding to entire classes of stimuli with classes of response. For example, once an individual has learned the rule connected with the red traffic signal he is able to respond by bringing any vehicle he is driving to a stop by any means at his disposal when any red signal is encountered. This behaviour is not simply the result of stimulus-response connections, although such connections will have been established at an earlier stage in the learning, but is rule governed and hence much more versatile in its application.

Problem solving comes at the top of Gagné's hierarchy. Problem solving is the process through which the learner draws upon his repertoire of previously learned rules in order to find a solution to a new problem. It amounts to more than just the application of previously acquired rules, for problem solving in its turn leads to new learning. When the individual is faced with a problem, according to Gagné, he formulates one or more hypotheses based upon the rules he has already learned; he then attempts to verify the hypotheses. Once an hypothesis is confirmed as correct it will be learned by being taken into the problem solver's repertoire of rules. The next time a comparable situation is encountered it will no longer be a problem, for the new rule will be available to bring about its prompt solution.

In Chapter 4 we will consider in more detail the way in which adults draw upon their past experience in problem solving and creative thought. At this point, however, it is worth noting that Gagné's learning hierarchy does make it easier to appreciate that there may be a natural progression from the random trial and error learning of Thorndike's cats to the insightful problem solving of Köhler's chimpanzees.

At each level of Gagné's learning hierarchy the learning that takes place draws upon the concepts of operant conditioning to account for the way in which the learning is established. From the feedback that comes from a successful performance at any level the learner receives reinforcement which increases the probability of the performance being repeated.

In this chapter we have briefly reviewed some of the major theoretical approaches to the study of learning. In the next four chapters we will turn our attention to the way in which adults learn different sorts of things, from facts and figures and problem solving strategies to sensori-motor and social skills.

3 LEARNING COGNITIVE INFORMATION

Learning and Organising New Verbal Information

A great deal of the material which we learn as adults, whether in a formal educational setting or as a result of the incidental learning that is an inevitable consequence of our routine activities, comes to us in verbal form. We attend to our teachers, read books and papers, listen to radio and television, consult instruction manuals and discuss matters with our friends. We sometimes learn from our own use of words; for example, when we write an essay or take part in a discussion we are often forced to organise our knowledge about a topic in a systematic and coherent way for the first time. In this chapter we will explore some of the work of psychologists which relates to the way we learn new verbal information and to the way we analyse verbal material and then go on to consider how we learn new concepts and how our new concepts are fitted into our existing conceptual structure.

The Analysis of Verbal Information

As we saw in the first chapter, when we are reading a book at a rate in excess of 200 words per minute we do not have the information processing capacity to take every word into our long-term memory. What we do is store the essential meaning of the material rather than its verbatim form. If we are asked to recall what we have read, then we will express the main ideas in our own words. It is this personal version of the material which constitutes our learning. This process of extracting the general sense of the verbal information that we encounter is what typically happens with adult verbal learning. There are, of course, some occasions when we are called upon to learn material verbatim; we may be learning a part in a play or mastering the highway code before taking a driving test. Even here we do not just register the sensory pattern of the words to be learned and reproduce them in the way a tape-recorder does, registering sound waves as a magnetic analogue which can be played back to produce a facsimile of the original sound. Instead we make use of the meaning and grammatical structure of the words to help us to code them for storage and to help in their recall from memory.

The learner, then, does not store verbal information in the long-term memory in the exact form in which it is encountered; instead it is analysed and translated into different forms for storage. We do not understand how this storage takes place from a physiological point of view, but from the psychological evidence it does seem that verbal information is stored in our long-term memory in a much condensed version of the original. The way in which we make our condensation of the new ideas for storage will be influenced by related ideas which we already have in store, as we shall see later in the chapter. When we need to recall the material in store we transform the condensed material back into an extended structure in sentences. These we then turn into written words or spoken sounds.

Craik and Lockhart (1972) have suggested that information is analysed at several levels as it is translated into the final form for storage in long-term memory. Take a word that is likely to be unfamiliar to most people such as 'mangonel'. How do we process such a word in preparing it for storage in long-term memory? Probably, initially it will be merely in terms of its appearance or its sound. This initial analysis is at the visual or auditory level. Now if we had first encountered the word in a sentence such as, 'The mangonel was positioned outside the wall', we could take our analysis of the word one stage further to the syntactic level. Although we may still not be able to give a definition of a mangonel we can at least recognise from its syntactical context that the word is a noun and hence it is the name of a person, place or object. If we then look up the word in a dictionary and discover that a mangonel is a medieval military engine for casting stones, our analysis of the word can then proceed to the semantic level, since we can now define the word mangonel. This semantic analysis can be in terms of either a verbal or imaginal definition. The dictionary definition of mangonel, for instance, gives only sufficient information for a verbal definition to be possible. We could not draw a mangonel with any degree of certainty as to its size or appearance from this definition.

With some words, however, we also have a clear visual image as a result of previous experience which is conjured up when we encounter them. The final level of analysis of a word, according to Craik and Lockhart, is concerned with our ability to accommodate it into our existing semantic memory. With the word mangonel the accommodation that is possible will vary greatly depending on the learner's past experience. If the learner is, for example, knowledgeable about early military technology and is already familiar with Roman military weapons, such as the ballista, then the new knowledge about the mangonel may well be fully integrated into memory alongside this existing knowledge. In this case the information may stand a strong chance of being retained for a long time in memory. On the other hand the word may be isolated, the only term of its kind and probably soon to be forgotten unless a great effort is made to establish it in long-term memory. The accommodation of new material can only come about when the learner already possesses related information in the long-term memory store to which the new material can be accommodated.

Our example suggests that the levels of analysis can range from little more than the registration of sensory stimulation up to the full understanding of new material and its accommodation into a complex network of other ideas. If this model of the processing of new information has any validity, we might expect that the higher the level at which the material is analysed then the longer the processing will take. An experiment by McMurray and Duffy (1972) has suggested that this is indeed the case. Students were timed as they learned twelve-letter strings of syllables which could be analysed either at the visual or auditory level only, or at this level and the semantic level. One list contained syllable strings that had no meaning for the subjects but which could be pronounced and so could only be processed as far as the auditory level. For example, NIC BUL GAN TAL. The other list contained meaningful abbreviations which could also be pronounced. These could be processed at both the auditory and the semantic levels. For example, RAF NUR AUG HON. The experimenters found that the mean time taken to learn the pronounceable string of syllables was 3.1 seconds, whereas the string that was both pronounceable and meaningful at the semantic level took an average 3.8 seconds to learn. One possible interpretation of these results is that the extra time taken to learn the meaningful material was due to the fact that the information was analysed to a higher level before it went forward for storage.

It may take longer to analyse isolated words through to the level at which they can be accommodated into the learner's existing knowledge but when a learner is confronted with a string of words or sentences to learn, far more can be retained when all the levels of analysis are available to the learner than when the material can only be analysed at a low level. For example, consider the problem that would face a non-German speaker asked to learn the following words — 'Ich wunsche euch eine fröhliche Weihnachten.' The analysis can only proceed to the auditory level and the amount of detail to be learned is considerable. However, for the German speaker who can analyse the sentence at the highest level and accommodate it into his existing knowledge it is no more difficult to learn than its English translation — 'I wish you a happy Christmas.' Material is analysed in terms of the learner's existing knowledge and this has very important implications for adult learning.

The Importance of Existing Knowledge

Bartlett (1932) suggested that the new learning is interpreted in terms of existing knowledge. He used an analogy from the neurological work of J. Head. Since we are able to recognise the change in position of a limb as the result of movement, the brain must have some way of registering the limb's previous position. This registration, based on previous sensory experience, Head called a schema (plural schemata). Bartlett borrowed this term and applied it to the learning of cognitive material. He conducted a whole series of experiments, many of them over a period of several years, which showed that when new cognitive material is encountered it is compared with what is already known in the existing schemata. In one of his experiments he got his subjects to read a passage of prose which recounted a North American Indian story. There were many features of the story, which told of the death of an Indian, that are peculiar to the cultural tradition of the American Indians. Bartlett found that many of the details that could not be accommodated within the subjects' schemata were lost when they were asked to recall the story at a later date. Likewise during the recall any gaps in the narrative that resulted from the failure to achieve accommodation of the culturally unfamiliar material were filled by drawing on the existing schemata of the subjects. This is the phenomenon which leads witnesses to 'invent' information when they are called upon to give evidence.

Piaget (1950) in his work also emphasises the way in which new material is assimilated by the learner who modifies it to fit the previously learned material which is stored in memory. In its turn the contents of the memory store become modified by the accommodation of the new material.

Meaningful and Rote Learning

Ausubel *et al.* (1978) also stress the influence on new learning of what the learner already knows, in his model of meaningful learning. He contrasts meaningful learning with rote learning. The essence of the meaningful learning process is that new ideas which are to be learned should be related to existing aspects of the learner's cognitive structure which are specifically relevant, such as an image, or an already meaningful symbol, concept or proposition. In rote memorisation on the other hand, definitions, concepts or propositions are learned by heart without any recognition of the meaning of the words in the definition. In Ausubel's view much material can be learned by either meaningful or rote learning depending on the past experience of the learner. For example, take the case of two students learning Ohm's Law: this states that the current in a circuit is directly proportional to the voltage. One student may learn by rote to reproduce the formula of words correctly but have no idea what they imply and no notion of how the formula has been derived or could be demonstrated. The other student may already have the concept of current, voltage, resistance and direct and inverse proportion meaningfully established in his long-term memory. When he encounters the formula of words of Ohm's Law he will be in a position to relate the formula to this already meaningful material. He will have learned something new and it will have been acquired in a meaningful way.

For meaningful learning to take place the learner must have relevant concepts available within his existing cognitive structure to which he can link the new material. An unconnected set of facts, of the kind that might be picked up from a quiz programme for example, will rapidly fade from memory. New information must fit into a structured pattern if it is to be successfully remembered. If that pattern can be made to relate to ideas that are already in the long-term memory store then so much the better. Perhaps the most important contribution a teacher can make to the adult's learning of cognitive information is to select, organise, present and translate new material in such a way that the learner can appreciate its relationship with ideas he already has clearly established in his memory. In this way the new ideas and information will stand the greatest chance of being retained in a clear, stable, and unambiguous form. They will become part of the integrated and organised body of knowledge in the mind of the adult learner.

So far in this chapter we have seen first, that the reception of new knowledge by a learner involves its analysis at various levels into forms that can be effectively stored in the long-term memory and secondly that at the highest level of analysis this processing is very strongly influenced by the knowledge which is already in store.

New Concepts and Existing Conceptual Structure

We will now go on to look in more detail at how the new information seems to be organised in the context of the existing material in long-term memory. This will involve us first in considering the way simple associations between a number of words are formed. Next we will look at the way in which new concepts are learned, and then we will consider the way in which individual concepts can be linked together to provide a conceptual structure which is at the heart of the individual's intellectual functioning.

The Learning of New Concepts

The simplest cognitive learning involves the formation of a link between two items. This is the verbal chain learning that R.M. Gagné places at the fourth level in his hierarchy of learning. We have a large number of these simple associations in our memory store. 'Thirty days hath September', 'In fourteen hundred and ninety-two, Columbus sailed the ocean blue', 'London is the capital of England', and 'Six sixes are thirty-six'. These simple associations can be rote learned and used without our having any real understanding of them. As an example many adults who learned their multiplication tables off by heart when they were small children will fail to realise that there are only two basic arithmetical processes, namely addition and subtraction. Multiplication is of course only cumulative addition. The verbal chain 'six sixes are thirty-six' is just a way of saying that if six sixes are added together they will come to a total of thirty-six.

For simple associations to be formed between words they must be presented very close together so that they can both be in the short-term memory at the same time and can then go forward into long-term memory. It is possible for the association to be established as the result of one presentation but normally the more frequently the association has been repeated the more durable it is likely to be in long-term memory. When there is no meaningful learning to support the establishment of an association then plenty of repetition and revision are called for. With plenty of practice, material which is rote learned will stay in memory for long periods. One of the problems with such rote learned material is that once it has been partially forgotten it cannot be reconstructed from other material in long-term memory. Whilst as adults we do engage in the learning of isolated simple associations, for example, learning the conversion formulae to change imperial into metric measures, most adult cognitive learning, whether formal or incidental, involves building upon a structure of existing concepts already within the long-term memory. If we rote learn the conversion formulae they will be useless to us if we forget any of the detail. If we learn them in a meaningful way, by understanding how the formulae are derived, then even if we forget part of the detail we will be able to draw on our other knowledge to reconstruct it.

As we saw in Chapter 1 the short term memory has a restricted capacity. The environment in which we live contains so much information that unless we had some way of organising it we would flounder in the immediate concrete situation and be quite unable to interpret it. We reduce this environmental complexity to manageable proportions by classifying and categorising. For example, the human eye is capable of discriminating between some seven million colour differences. However, we use only a very limited number of colour concepts. By automatically categorising whole ranges of subtly different colours under the concept blue we greatly reduce the amount of learning that we would otherwise have to engage in.

Concept Formation

Concepts reduce the amount of information that we have to deal with and this makes our thinking and long-term retention of our past experience vastly easier than if we were attempting to deal with the raw sensory data that reach us from the environment. A concept is a system of learned responses which enable us to organise and interpret data. Our concepts are usually associated with specific words or phrases, but it is possible to have concepts without verbal labels to identify them. There are numerous ways in which we group data together to form concepts. Probably the simplest is on the basis of physical identity or similarity amongst the instances. For example, we may think of 'car' as a concept. Here the various observable characteristics of a particular variety of motor vehicle serve as the common features. Consider the concept 'vegetable'; there is very little physical similarity between a tomato or lettuce, a carrot or a pumpkin, but the use to which each is put links them together. Other bases for grouping, less obvious and more complex, are often used, but whatever the underlying principle is, it is usually logical, rational and understandable.

Grouping things together implies in some sense at least that all members of the group are responded to in the same way; for adults this response is often wholly, or in part, verbal. It is important, however, to recognise that the same stimulus object can be grouped under more than one concept. For example, a pumpkin may be grouped under any of the following concepts: vegetable, food, fruit, cucurbit-aeceous plant, gourd or pie filling. Each of these concepts will have other instances besides pumpkin. When any of these individual concepts is in use to categorise the pumpkin, the response towards the pumpkin will be like that made to other examples of the concept. A pumpkin conceived of as a gourd will call forth responses different to those produced by the pumpkin as a pie filling. Concepts that involve grouping similar items under a common name or category are called class concepts.

Concepts do not exist in nature, they are a product of man's intellect. We make a decision to group a range of plants under the concept 'tree' whilst other, not dissimilar plants are grouped under the concept 'shrub'. The Eskimo who lives in an environment that may be permanently snow covered has no single concept 'snow'. Such a concept would not be precise enough for his needs; instead he has separate concepts for powdered snow, for hard-packed snow or slushy snow and so on. Such concepts help him respond more effectively to his environment. Concepts can enable us to respond effectively to the complexity of the world. The scientist, the technician or the academic have a mastery over a particular subject discipline which the rest of us lack because they have a considerably richer conceptual structure within the area of concern of the discipline. Because he has mastered the concept of his discipline the chemist is able to plan and control chemical processes of great complexity to produce new plastics or man made fibres. Those of us who lack his conceptual framework may view his work and see no more than attractively coloured liquids in glass beakers.

The key to understanding a subject is to understand its concepts. These concepts are identified by words. If all the words that are connected with say chemistry or history or theology could be removed from the language then it would not be too far fetched to say that chemistry, history and theology could no longer exist. To know a subject is to know the meanings attached to the words that represent its concepts.

How are new concepts formed? Suppose we are showing a friend who is quite ignorant about flowers and their names around the garden. We come to a mixed bed of dahlias. No two dahlias growing here are identical, either the flower shape or its size or its colour varies, but there are a number of attributes which all the plants have to a greater or lesser degree. They all have leaves of a very similar shape and colour. The height of the plants varies but the general pattern of growth of all the plants has much in common. If some of the flowers have gone to seed we can point to the similarity amongst the seed heads. We might dig up a couple of the plants to show our friend that they all grow from tubers under the ground. We may also draw his attention to the distinctive smell that comes from the bruised dahlia foliage. Although there are differences amongst the flowers, all the flowers fall into one of ten groups which vary according to the shape and formation of the flower and petal, and the size of the bloom. By presenting the various instances and by giving verbal guidance we help our friend abstract out from the range of dahlias he has seen the relevant attributes of 'dahlianess'. In his mind he begins to form the concept of dahlia. If he has successfully attained the concept from our guidance and instruction then the next time he comes upon a bed of flowers he should be able to discriminate between dahlias and other flowers.

Once a concept has been learned then we can apply it or generalise it on to new instances that share the same essential attributes. Through our acquisition of concepts, from the simplest class concepts to complex moral, aesthetic and scientific concepts, we gain intellectual mastery over the complexity of the environment. Acquiring a new concept, then, involves learning the relevant attributes of the concept, either by abstracting these attributes for oneself from a number of instances of the concept, or from a verbal description of the attributes. In most practical learning situations a combination of both approaches is used. This is because the verbal definition of many concepts is far from easy and everyone finds it easier to understand complex verbal statements when they can be related to practical instances. Think of the problems in giving a verbal description of the attributes of such a familiar concept as 'dog' so as to exclude wolves, hyenas and foxes.

Strategies in Concept Attainment

In formal learning settings new concepts are usually taught by giving a verbal description of the concept in terms of the relevant attributes together with instances of the concept, if this is possible. When we are left to work out the attributes of a concept for ourselves, as, for example, might happen if we were trying to discover from a number of instances which claimants were and which claimants were not entitled to free dental treatment under the National Health Service, we do not all use the same strategies. Bruner carried out a series of experiments which investigated the different strategies that people used in concept-attainment tasks (Bruner *et al.*, 1956). He found that people adopted one of two broad plans of action. He called these scanning and focusing strategies. With a scanning strategy the learner begins by framing one or more hypotheses about part of the first example of the concept that he encounters. He bets on one or more features of the example as the defining attributes for the concept. As long as future examples continue to show these attributes he maintains his hypothesis or hypotheses. He also sticks to his hypothesis or hypotheses as long as non-examples do not have the attribute or attributes. If he comes across an example that contradicts an hypothesis then he has to change it by looking for a new one that will be consistent with all the positive instances encountered up to that point. When the learner tries to scan with all the possibilities in mind Bruner calls it simultaneous scanning. This strategy is very difficult, for the learner needs to deal with many independent hypotheses and to carry them all in his memory. The alternative is to scan with one hypothesis in mind at a time; this is called successive scanning. It greatly reduces the difficulty of the task but it is not far short of trial and error learning.

With the focusing strategy the learner takes the first positive instance of the concept he encounters and makes it the basis of his initial hypothesis. If he meets a contradictory instance of his hypothesis then he must take what is common to the initial hypothesis and the contradictory instance and ignore everything else.

In his experiments Bruner found that the majority of his subjects chose a focusing strategy to arrive at the definitive attributes of the concepts. The advantage of focusing is that it maximises the information gained at each step and reduces the load on the learner's memory and powers of inference to a minimum; it is particularly useful when time is limited. Bruner found that when his subjects were working under timed conditions 63 per cent of those using focusing strategies were successful compared with only 37 per cent of the scanners.

Bruner's work was carried out under experimental conditions. Real-life concept learning is perhaps not adequately represented by the experimental materials but nonetheless Bruner's work does throw very interesting light on the different approaches that adults may take to the attainment of new concepts in everyday life.

Relevant and Irrelevant Attributes of Concepts

When we learn a new concept we need to know which attributes are relevant and which irrelevant. In the case of our non-gardening friend learning the new class concept of dahlia, we were at pains to draw his attention to the relevant attributes. There were, however, a number of other attributes of the dahlias which were not relevant to the acquisition of the concept. Dahlia flowers come in a wide range of colours, some flowers are single coloured, some have a range of hues.

Colour of flower is an irrelevant attribute in the acquisition of this particular concept. Likewise colour, make and model, engine position, number of doors and seats, position of the steering wheel and kerbside weight are all irrelevant attributes of the class concept of motor car for they do not help to define the concept.

There are three main factors which influence the ease with which a new concept is attained. These are the number of relevant attributes that must be learned, the number of irrelevant attributes that may cause interference and the degree of similarity that exists between the new concept and the others that are being learned or are already in long-term memory.

Using university undergraduates as his subjects, Schvanevelat (1966) explored the effect of varying between one and four the number of relevant dimensions required in order to learn a concept which in each case had two irrelevant dimensions. The concepts to be learned had as their attributes the positions of lines which were added to a cross shape. Schvanevelat found that there was a linear relationship between the number of relevant attributes to the concept and the number of presentations that were necessary before it was learned. The more relevant the attributes, the longer it took to attain. The same conclusion, not surprisingly, holds for irrelevant attributes; the greater the number of irrelevant attributes the more difficult it is to master the concept.

Similarity between concepts can also cause problems for the learner. The similarity between concepts depends on the number of relevant attributes that they share in common. The more relevant the attributes two concepts share the more difficult a learner is likely to find it to discriminate between one concept and the other. It is more difficult to discriminate between a butterfly and a moth than between a butterfly and a bee.

So far in this chapter we have considered some of the factors associated with the learning of class concepts. Many subjects that adult learners may study will involve them in learning specific concepts. For example, some readers of this book may have encountered the specific concept Ivan Pavlov for the first time in an earlier chapter. The concept 'Ivan Pavlov' refers to a particular person and the reader may have already linked a number of relevant attributes to his name. For instance: born 1849, lived and worked in Russia, physiologist, experimented on dogs, identified classical conditioning, died 1936. Specific concepts are attained in very much the same way as class concepts with relevant attributes becoming attached to the concept label.

The Organisation of Conceptual Structure

Concepts do not exist in isolation in long-term memory as we have already discovered. Let us now explore in more detail how our conceptual structure may be organised. Some concepts are linked with others because they can all be subsumed under another concept. For example, oak, elm, beech, spruce, larch and pine can all be linked under the more inclusive class concept of tree. Some concepts are dependent upon others for their definition and are linked together for that reason; for example the volt is defined in terms of the ampere and ohm. Both forms of organisation seem to be used in structuring the concepts in our long-term memory.

Bousefield (1953) presented university undergraduates with a randomised list of 60 words drawn from four different categories of class concepts, namely animals, names, professions and vegetables. Immediately following the presentation the subjects were asked to list the items they were able to recall. The items that were recalled were often clustered together in their conceptual categories, animals with animals, names with other names and so on, rather than in the randomised order in which they had been presented. These results suggest that the subjects had ordered the random words under headings that already existed in the long-term memory.

Collins and Quillian (1969) explained the way concepts are organised in a hierarchical fashion in more detail. In order to check the truth of a statement such as 'A canary can fly' we need to draw upon information which is stored in our long-term memory. There are two possible ways in which this information might be organised. One way would be to store alongside the name of every bird the fact that it can fly, i.e., sparrows can fly, larks can fly, canaries can fly and so on. In this case in order to check on the accuracy of the statement we would need to see if an appropriate fact was stored alongside the name of the bird. An alternative way to organise the information would be to store the information in a hierarchical fashion. In this case it would only be necessary to store the fact that birds can fly, we could then draw the inference that a canary can fly from the stored information that a canary is a bird and birds can fly.

According to this hierarchical model each concept has stored alongside it in long-term memory those attributes which are exclusive to it. However, those attributes which it shares with other concepts belonging to the same class or category will be stored higher up in the hierarchy. A canary is yellow and can sing; these particular attributes will be stored with the concept canary. A sparrow is gregarious and chirps in a monotone; these attributes will be stored with sparrow. But that they both have feathers, can fly and lay eggs will be stored higher up the hierarchy with the more inclusive concept bird. Collins and Quillian call these higher level concepts super-sets. At a higher level still under the more inclusive concept, or super-set, of animal will be stored attributes such as the facts that they, along with other animals, breathe, move, eat and have skin.

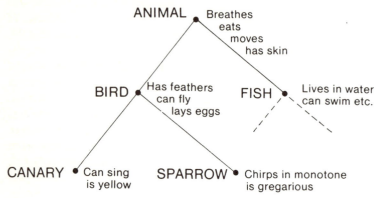

(After Collins & Quillian 1969)

The advantage of this way of organising the conceptual contents of our long-term memory is that it is much more economical in terms of the storage space required. The fact that any animal can breathe would only need to be stored once alongside animal rather than separately with every variety of animal of which we can think. Collins and Quillian argued that if this model is a valid one then it should be possible to test it by seeing whether there was any variation in the time it took to confirm statements that required inferences to be drawn from different levels of the hierarchy. They found that statements about category membership took longer to confirm the further they were apart in the hierarchy. For example, it took 1.00 second to confirm that a canary is a canary, 1.17 seconds to confirm that a canary is a bird and 1.24 seconds to confirm that a canary is an animal. They also found that the time that it took to confirm the attributes varied depending upon the level at which these attributes were stored. For example, it took 1.31 seconds to confirm that a canary can sing, an attribute that would be stored with the concept canary, but 1.47 seconds to confirm that a canary has skin, an attribute which would probably be stored higher in the hierarchy as a characteristic of all animals. The fact that attributes take rather longer to locate than category membership adds further confirmation to the hierarchical model for conceptual organisation that Collins and Quillian advance.

Even looking at the limited range of concepts outlined above it is clear from our own experience that the diagram represents only the sketchiest outline of the way in which the concepts that we have are distinguished and interrelated. For example, we know far more about sparrows than that they are gregarious and chirp in monotones. We can probably distinguish between male and female sparrows, and between house sparrows and field sparrows. We know what kind of food they eat and that they use twigs and waste material to build nests. Our cognitive structure will have developed and grown as a consequence of our learning and experience. Everyone will have differences in the way material is organised in long-term memory. No one is yet in a position to begin to suggest just how involved and complicated the internal structures of the human mind must be. It would appear that verbal material is stored in a hierarchical way. The hierarchy of ideas and concepts within the human mind will have developed as the result of the experiences of the individual. As each individual will have had many experiences that are unique to him then we must expect individuals to differ in the organisation of the concepts in their long-term memory and this of course has implications for the way that new ideas are assimilated. A new idea or concept that can be readily related or assimilated to something that is in long-term memory already, will be more easily retained than material which is quite new and being encountered for the very first time.

In this chapter we have concentrated on the way verbal material is learned and integrated into our conceptual structure but language is only one of the ways in which our thought may be organised. Action and images also have their place in our cognitive structure. Plans for carrying out the sequences of action involved in a skill are almost certainly organised in a hierarchical fashion. We still do not know enough about the workings of our mind to even be confident that the network of interrelations in our cognitive structure involves the use of language at all. What is certain, however, is that the most important single factor influencing new adult learning is what the learner has learned already and has organised in his conceptual structure.

4 LEARNING COGNITIVE STRATEGIES

The Process of Problem Solving

The Contexts of Problem Solving

In many contexts in adult life people find themselves having to tackle new tasks which are slightly different from those that they have encountered before. No two classes are ever quite the same for a teacher, no two seasons identical for the farmer. In many occupations such as engineering, medicine or equipment repair and servicing, being able to respond to new problems with a strategy which is based on previous experience is at the heart of what the effective practitioner does. In this chapter we will consider some of the evidence on how people come to tackle cognitive tasks, particularly those involving problem solving, through the acquisition and exploitation of cognitive strategies, rules or plans.

It is very rare indeed in our day to day lives that we encounter two situations that are completely identical and which call forth identical responses from us. Most of the time we find that although we have knowledge which is relevant to the situation or task that we are faced with, we none the less need to use this knowledge in a subtly different way from the way we have used it in the past. For example, if we sit down to write a series of thank you letters, each letter will follow a general format but each will differ depending on the recipient. The housewife planning what to give the family to eat will have faced this particular problem many times before but on every occasion there will be some special circumstance such as a member of the family feeling off colour, a glut of vegetables, or perhaps some constraint of time or cost which will mean that last week's solution to the problem will not do. The motorist will need to carry out a slightly different sequence of responses on every trip no matter how familiar the route. In the formal educational setting the learner may be required to design and conduct an experiment or to write an essay to evaluate a proposition. In each of these circumstances there are some aspects of the task which will have close similarities to tasks that have been carried out before, but there will be another element which is unique to the task in hand and which presents the learner with a problem that he has never encountered before in quite that form. All of these situations, and many more besides, present the individual with a problem or series of problems which need to be solved. How do we solve such problems?

Reproductive and Productive Thinking

There seem to be two major strategies which we may employ when faced with a problem. If it can be seen to have many similarities with situations which we have successfully tackled in the past, then we will almost certainly adapt the strategy which we employed previously. In most cases this will be likely to lead to a rapid and efficient solution. Maier (1945) called the thinking in this kind of situation, where the solution is reached through the direct application of previous learning, reproductive thought. Reproductive thinking is closely similar if not identical to the transfer of training which we will consider in the next chapter in connection with skills. If the problem with which we are faced appears to be a novel one or at least appears to have a large number of novel elements, then we are likely to engage in what Maier terms productive thinking. In productive thinking we repattern and restructure our past experience in order to meet the special circumstances of the current situation. We have available to us a whole repertoire of strategies for problem solving that we have acquired in the past and it is to these that we turn first when faced with a new problem.

Gagne sees the strategies which we adopt to solve problems as depending on the rules we have available. For Gagne (1977) the problem solving process involves the learner in discovering how a combination of previously learned rules can be applied in order to achieve a solution to a novel situation. Problem solving though is not merely a question of applying rules that have been previously learned, for the problem solving process may also yield new learning. The new and original solution to a problem will be retained by the learner as a new higher-order rule which will be available next time a similar problem is encountered. Gagne places learning through problem solving behaviour at the top of his learning hierarchy. When the individual is engaged in the application of already existing rules to the solution of a problem he is engaged in reproductive thought; when he is tackling a new problem for which no rules are readily available he is engaged in productive thought. The new rules which result from the productive thought will be stored to be utilised at a later date in reproductive thought.

Plans and the Control of Behaviour

Whilst Gagne talks of rules as the building bricks for problem solving,

Miller, Galanter and Pribram (1960) use the term 'plan' to describe very much the same thing. For them a plan is any hierarchical process that can control the order in which a sequence of operations is to be performed. Human behaviour is very largely controlled by the plans for action that we have developed as the result of our past learning. The plans of the individual are very much the same as the programme of a computer. When we successfully solve a problem for the first time we will have worked out a plan for its solution according to Miller, Galanter and Pribram.

The term plan can be used to describe the general strategy that we may adopt to tackle a problem before the details have been worked out as well as to describe the detailed specification of every stage of the operations to be performed. Once we have evolved a plan to tackle a problem then we will be likely to store the plan in long-term memory so that it can be utilised on future occasions when an identical or similar problem is encountered again. In most occupational fields, it is generally accepted that the older, more experienced person tends to be more effective in solving complex and subtle problems than his younger, less experienced colleagues. Almost certainly any such differences that do exist will be due, at least in some part, to the greater repertoire of pre-existent plans which the more experienced person has at his command. Plans are essential to our efficient performance in everyday situations. Once we have formulated a plan and found it successful then it can be stored in long-term memory and used time and time again. When we solve a fresh problem the plan that we evolve can be stored for use on future occasions.

The Process of Problem Solving

Let us look at the process of problem solving in more detail. In the first place whether we have plans available or not, we must be able to recognise and identify the problem. Not until the problem has been defined does it really exist in a form that is capable of solution. If we only know in a vague way that our car has come to a halt and will no longer go we can have no idea whether we have any plans or strategies that will enable us to deal with the problem. What we need to do is to explore the field in which the problem exists. We may merely review in a passive way all the information that is to hand. For example, what do we know of the car's performance before it came to a stop? Were the lights dim, was the engine overheating, were there unusual noises from the gear box or did the brakes perform strangely? Each of these characteristics would suggest different causes of the problem. We may actively explore the possible causes. For example, check the oil and water levels and test the battery and so on. From these actions and observations we are likely to begin to form a number of hypotheses about the possible cause of the problem and we will then attempt to evaluate the evidence that supports or contradicts these hypotheses. This is a period for much apparent trial and error activity and working things through mentally.

To identify a problem successfully is often to solve it. If we find that the car will not start because there is corrosion at the battery terminal or because the starter motor is jammed then we may well have a sequence of strategies or plans for action already in our repertoire of behaviour which will enable us to solve the problem at once. We engage in Maier's reproductive thinking.

Problem Solving and Set

Although the analysis of a problem in such a way that some previously mastered plan or strategy can be called upon is usually an advantage, there are occasions when being set in our ways and using the well tried solution may prevent our solving a problem or lead us to solve it in a less efficient fashion. If we have always paid our bills by sending postal orders, then we may never get round to using the bank giro transfer service although it would be cheaper and easier. This set, as it is called, is the opposite of originality because it exists on occasions when the problem solver does not think of a new way to do things. Sets are very common in everyday life. A temporary set is produced by the starter's instructions before a race 'get ready, get set, go!' We may become set to buy a particular brand of cigarette and will not consider any other. We may be set to read a book from the first chapter straight through although for academic study this may not be the most effective way to read it. The characteristic of behaviour that we call set is that we do not stop to think about what we are doing. If we have correctly identified the situation as a familiar one for which we already have an effective sequence of behaviour available, this may be the most efficient way of operating but sometimes being set leads us to perform inefficiently.

Luchins (1942) demonstrated how set can interfere with the efficient solution of problems. He gave a group of college staff, graduate students and research workers a series of eleven problems to solve. In each problem they were asked to obtain an exact amount of water given three empty jars of stated capacities as their measures. For example, the second problem asked for 100 quarts to be obtained using empty jars of 21, 127 and 3 quarts capacity. After 2½ minutes the subjects were asked for their solutions and the answer was illustrated in both written and verbal form. The method which solved the second problem also solved problems three to six. If we designate the jars as A, B and C respectively, the solution to these problems may be described as B - A - 2C. This formula of B - A - 2C could also be used to solve the seventh, eighth, tenth and eleventh problems, however these four problems and problem nine could all be solved more easily and economically using the formula A - C.

Luchins found that his subjects experienced set and all persisted in using the more circuitous method B - A - 2C to solve problems seven and eight. Problem nine could only be solved using the formula A - C, none the less all but 15 per cent of the subjects continued to use the less efficient B - A - 2C formula for problems ten and eleven. A reliance on plans that have been effective in the past, then, may hinder creative thought. The flexible thinker is one who can approach a new problem with his existing repertoire of plans available, but who can develop a new and more efficient way to solve the problem if it is possible.

Strategies for Productive Thought

So far we have looked at problem solving where reproductive thinking can be called upon, where a well tried plan or strategy can be utilised as soon as its appropriateness has been recognised. Let us now turn our attention to the situation where we do not have a readily available repertoire of plans that can be utilised in solving the problem that faces us. What factors seem to influence success in productive thought? Duncker (1945) carried out a number of experiments from which we can draw some useful conclusions about the ways in which people search for the solution to a problem. As we have already seen, the first step towards solving a problem involves identifying the relevant aspects of the problem, so that possible hypotheses can be formulated. Suppose with our broken down car we have noted that the engine seemed to bind before it eventually came to a halt, we may correctly diagnose that it stopped because it had overheated from some cause. Our first hypothesis may be that a radiator hose has split and that the water that normally cools the engine has escaped. On investigation we may discover the water level is normal in the radiator and that indeed the water is rather cool. The mistaken solution put forward is however not unhelpful, we have eliminated one hypothesis and gained some fresh information that may contribute to a reformulation of the problem.The engine has overheated although the cooling system is intact. One of our next hypotheses, that the coolant has not circulated either because of a fault in the water pump, or because of the fan belt not working properly, is confirmed when we discover the fan belt is missing.

Duncker found that each proposal put forward involved a re-formulation of the problem. The basis of each new hypothesis is a shifting of the relationship between the factors which make up the problem. Hypotheses are evaluated on their functional appropriateness. With some problems a number of alternatives may be equally appropriate as functional solutions. Once hypotheses which are sound from a functional point of view have been brought out then it will be practical considerations which will determine which solution will be implemented. Having discovered the fan belt has broken we will try to solve the problem of how to get the car on the go again by looking for a suitable substitute. Amongst the objects in the back of the car we may find a length of electric flex, a piece of cord and an old nylon stocking. Here are three possible means of replacing the broken belt. We would probably first try the cord as the functions that we normally associate with cord are closer to those of the belt than the functions we normally associate with electric flex and nylon stockings. Duncker draws attention to the idea of available functions. If the only function that comes to mind for a nylon stocking is for it to grace a lady's leg, then it will not occur to us to use it in solving a problem where, say, a rope or a filter are required. If, however, we have experience of old nylon stockings being used to tie up a bundle of sticks or to filter petrol, then we will have these functions available for the stocking and may quickly formulate a plan making use of the stocking in its less familiar function to solve the problem.

Availability of Functions and Problem Solving

Saugstad and Raaheim (1960) explored the way in which the availability of functions influenced problem solving in 17-year-old boys studying science in a secondary school. The aim of their experiment was to discover whether experiences necessary for the solution of a problem can be conveyed to subjects. They demonstrated in advance the rather unfamiliar functions certain objects needed to have if a particular problem was to be solved.

The problem required each subject in turn to transfer a number of steel balls from a glass into a metal cylinder. The glass containing the steel balls was placed on a movable wooden frame and the metal cylinder was placed to the side of it. The boy had to keep behind a table

260 cm away from the wooden frame. In order to tackle the problem the boy was provided with four newspapers, a length of string, a pair of pliers, five elastic bands and a nail. This may not seem like a very promising set of equipment but the problem can be solved by bending the nail into a hook with the pliers, attaching the nail to the string and then fishing for the wooden frame which has the glass of steel balls on it. Once the steel balls have been hauled in, the newspapers need to be rolled into a continuous tube held together with the elastic bands. This tube is used to direct the steel balls into the metal cylinder. The 20 boys in the experimental group were asked to think of as many functions as they could for a nail as a hook and to think of as many functions as possible for a newspaper as a tube. The experimenters allowed the boys 30 minutes in which to solve the problem and 19 of them were successful. There were 45 boys in the control group who did not have these critical functions drawn to their attention and only 10 of these solved the problem in the 30 minutes available. It is clear from this experiment that having the relevant functions of objects available in the long-term memory store contributes greatly to the effectiveness with which the individual can formulate a plan to solve an unfamiliar problem. The boys who had not had the opportunity to consider some of the more unusual functions for the objects which they had available were far less successful than the experimental group in solving the problem. Those who did find a solution were much slower than the experimental group.

Productive thinking cannot take place when there is nothing for the problem solver to work on. The creative solution to a problem involves combining previous experiences together in a new way. As Gagné's hierarchy of learning emphasises, our success in solving problems depends on the prior acquisition of a wide variety of knowledge and experience. The adult who is required to solve problems must be given the chance to acquire the necessary background material first.

The part which is played by past experience in human problem solving behaviour is, however, far from clear-cut. Whilst the above experiment demonstrates the advantages of being exposed to the possibilities of objects being used with novel functions, an experiment by Birch and Rabinowitz (1951) demonstrated the negative effect which previous experience can have upon productive thinking. They worked with 25 engineering students in a college. They divided them into three groups, a control group and two experimental groups. One experimental group was required to complete an electrical circuit using a switch, the other experimental group completed an identical circuit using a relay. The control group were given no experience with either switch or relay. Shortly after completing the circuits all the subjects in turn were asked to solve a problem which required them to tie together the free ends of two cords suspended from the ceiling to the floor. The distance between the cords was too great for the subject to reach one cord whilst the other was held. The solution to the problem required the subject to tie a weight to the end of one of the cords in order to convert it into a pendulum. The stationary cord could be held and the pendulum caught on the upswing. The two cords could then be tied together. In the experiment the only two objects available that were suitable as weights for the pendulum were the electrical switch and the relay used earlier in making the circuits.

The control group chose equally between switch and the relay in the solutions to the two cord task, but of the subjects who had the pre-test experience with the relay, 100 per cent chose the switch as the pendulum weight. Of the group who had formed the circuit using the switch, 78 per cent chose the relay for the pendulum weight. When the data from the two experimental groups were combined it was found that 90 per cent of the subjects had solved the problem using the object they had not used in the electrical circuit. Equipment which had been used in an electrical context could not readily be seen as having another function such as acting as a weight.

Functional Fixedness

Duncker (1945) called this inability to see the full potential of objects functional fixedness. The previous use of an object in a function dissimilar to that required in the new task inhibits the discovery of the possibility of a new use for the object. It would appear that functional fixedness influenced the subjects' responses in the above experiment. The pre-problem solving experience with the electrical circuit apparently changed the perceived properties of the switch or the relay to such an extent that their other characteristics could no longer be readily seen. Something which had just been used as an electrical object became difficult to see in terms of its more general characteristic of mass. The experience limited the number of functions of the object that the subject could perceive.

Past experience in relation to productive thinking can either facilitate problem solving as in the case of the Saugstad and Raaheim experiment, by helping the problem solver become aware of a wider range of available functions, or it may reduce the range of possible uses which the problem solver can envisage for objects through the effects of functional fixedness. It seems that it is how and what the problem solver has learned in the past, rather than whether he has learned, which determines the extent of the positive transfer that will occur on to new problem solving tasks.

The Phases of Problem Solving

As we have seen, previous learning experience has a crucial role to play in problem solving. We cannot produce new and creative solutions out of thin air. Polya (1945) has distinguished four phases in problem solving. First, we must understand the nature of the problem. We need to be able to identify the relevant information that the problem contains. We need to be able to recognise the constraints of possible solutions and we need to try to identify what it is we are looking for in a solution. Past learning will influence how effectively we can do this. Secondly, we must work out a plan that will enable us to connect the information that we do have with unknown aspects of the problem. At this stage we will draw upon our store of plans in long-term memory. If no plan is available we will need to explore the functions available for different aspects of the problem. At this stage we need to be wary of set or functional fixedness interfering with our efficiency. This second stage is the most critical. The third phase involves us in carrying through the plan we have recalled or evolved. Each step needs to be checked as we go to ensure that our solution is working out effectively. If our evaluation of our progress leads us to suspect that something is going awry then we must modify our plan or even reassess the nature of the problem. The fourth phase involves evaluation; we must look back over the completed solution, identify its strengths and weaknesses and perhaps think of improvements upon it for future occasions. The evaluative phase is important for our future success in solving comparable problems for it provides us with the plans for future reproductive thought. Once stored in long-term memory, plans that have been successful in the past become available as solutions for comparable problems when they are encountered in the future.

Problem Solving and Age

There is some evidence from problem solving experiments that have been carried out on samples of adults chosen to give a cross-section of age ranges, that as people grow older problem solving becomes less effective. Unfortunately it is difficult to interpret these data because the older subjects may well have had poorer educational opportunities than the younger adults. In spite of these reservations, there are some characteristics of the less efficient problem solving strategies of the older learner which can usefully be identified. Older subjects seem to have a more pronounced tendency to repeat their non-productive strategies and to repeat non-informative enquiries when they are attempting to identify the nature of the problem. The difficulties which older people have with interference to short-term memory can make it more difficult for them to handle the information relevant to finding a solution. Older people also have a greater tendency to try a re-run of the plans and strategies that have worked for them in the past even though they are inappropriate to the problem that faces them. They also have a tendency to misinterpret information that indicates they are on the wrong track, they often interpret it as confirming that they are right. This puts off the disappointment and anxiety that may go with recognising that they are wrong but it also delays finding a successful solution (Jerome, 1962). Perhaps a more heartening finding comes from a longitudinal study carried out by Arenberg (1974) who followed up the same individuals over a period of six years. He found age only began to affect problem solving behaviour in a significant way after the age of seventy.

Most of the experimental studies on adult problem solving have used artificial problem solving tasks in order to minimise the influence of past experience. In everyday life adults normally enlarge their repertoire of plans for the solution of problems as the years pass. Older adults seem mainly to search their existing repertoire to find solutions for problems, relying on reproductive thinking rather than generating new solutions. Adult problem solving in general is likely to become more effective over the years as a greater repertoire of solutions is amassed, but when novel solutions needing productive thought are required the older adult may perform less efficiently than he did in the past (Birren, 1964).

5   LEARNING SKILLS

The Nature of Skill

So far we have concentrated our attention mainly on the way in which cognitive material is learned. A great deal of adult learning does involve the acquisition of new facts and ideas. As we saw in the last chapter, these are exploited when we tackle problems which are new to us. In this chapter we will turn our attention to slightly different ground, to the way in which we, as adults, acquire new skills.

All skills, whether they are industrial skills or the skills of day to day life, whether they involve physical activity or are predominantly mental, have a number of characteristics in common. All are learned, all involve the building up of organised and co-ordinated activities in relation to some specific object or event, and all involve the ordering and co-ordination of a number of different processes or actions in a temporal sequence. They are serial in nature, that is to say one activity follows on from another.

The human capacity to learn skills is very great; we begin at birth as we slowly learn to co-ordinate our bodily movements, painfully master walking and then go on to acquire yet more skills involving body, hand and eye co-ordination that enable us to eat our food and play with our toys. By the time we reach adulthood we have acquired a repertoire of thousands of different skills. They may range from cleaning our teeth to driving a car, writing, playing a musical instrument, dealing with social situations or operating the complex products of technology. As the circumstances of our life change, we master fresh skills to cope with them. All our skills, whether physical, mental or social involve us in making appropriate learned responses that are intended to achieve a predictable result with the maximum certainty of success and minimum expenditure of time and effort.

Physiological and Psychological Processes in Skilled Performance

There are both physiological and psychological processes involved in performing any skill. Amongst its many functions the human nervous system receives information from the immediate evironment, processes the information, makes decisions about its significance and then, when necessary, causes suitable bodily actions to be taken as the result of the decisions made. We have already encountered some aspects of the monitoring and decision-making mechanisms in our consideration of the sensory, short-term and long-term stages of memory. The receptor, central decision-making and effector mechanisms in the shape of the sense receptors, nerve fibres, brain and muscles are 'wired in' as part of the physiological structure of the mature individual. The interpretation of the significance of incoming sensory information, the decision-making and the successful execution of the appropriate physical manoeuvres all involve a psychological dimension; all are dependent upon past experience and all have to be learned. When as a result of previous learning, a person can successfully interpret relevant information that comes to him from an aspect of the environment and can take appropriate, efficient action he can be described as skilled in that particular area.

The receptor processes provide the input of sensory information. In performing the many skills of adult life we make much greater use of the information from our senses than we probably ever realise. Besides the traditional five senses of sight, hearing, touch, taste and smell there is a very important sixth sense which provides us with proprioceptive information, that is to say information from within our body. It is known as the kinaesthetic sense. All our senses are involved in one skill or another but without our kinaesthetic sense none of the carefully controlled physical movements which are the characteristic of so many skills would be possible.

The kinaesthetic sense provides us with information about the movement and positioning of our body and limbs. The information comes from sensory nerve endings in muscles, tendons and joints and it enables us to tell when, as a result of muscular contraction, a movement has been made or pressure has been exerted in some way. The tennis player uses his kinaesthetic sense to judge whether the racquet is moving with the right velocity and at the right angle to return the ball with the speed and the flight path that he intends. The car driver uses his kinaesthetic sense to judge the right pressures to exert with his feet to balance the clutch and the accelerator as he prepares to drive off in his car. The kinaesthetic sense enables us to make the fine movements involved in writing with a pen. Although the kinaesthetic sense is often overlooked, like the senses of sight and touch it is one of our primary sources of sensory information for almost every skill we perform. Hearing is not so often a primary source of information but it often has a very important secondary role to play. For example, when playing tennis, sight, kinaesthesis and touch are the primary sources of relevant information, none the less the experienced player may learn much about the speed and probable degree of spin his opponent has imparted to the ball from the sound of the ball hitting the racquet. Likewise the car driver makes considerable use of the information that comes from the sounds of the engine, the tyres and the other vehicles on the road. Sound can often provide us with a warning of what is happening in parts of the environment that we cannot immediately see.

Limits to Processing Information

The sensory input that has its origins in the stimulation of the sense receptors is conveyed to the brain via the sensory nerve system. Exactly how this sensory input is processed and the decisions made about the motor output is only very partially understood. The human ability to process information is limited. We have already seen, in earlier chapters, how these limitations affect the way in which we memorise. There is considerable evidence that the human nervous system functions like a single-channel communication system with a limited capacity for taking in, storing, processing and acting upon information (Welford, 1968). This model implies that anyone performing a skill can only cope with one meaningfully organised chunk of information at a time. This information needs to be dealt with before fresh information can be attended to. Some writers would challenge this single-channel view (Legge and Barber, 1976). No one, however, would dispute the reality of the limit on our ability to process information.

As we become more skilled we learn to select the sensory input we will attend to in such a way that we can get the maximum information from the minimum input. This is one of the strategies that we adopt to cope with the limits on our capacity to process information. The skilled driver, for example, just glances in his driving mirror and can assess the future movements of the cars behind him. The novice driver, when he looks in the mirror, is not sure what cues he is looking for and so attends to more information than is relevant to his needs.

The limit on our capacity to process information is illustrated by an experiment with highly skilled car drivers (Brown, 1962). The drivers were given auditory recognition tasks to perform and a check was kept of their rate of success. When the drivers were progressing along quiet residential roads where the number of potential hazards that they had to monitor was small, they were able to tackle considerably more tasks than when they were driving in a town shopping area under more demanding conditions. As experienced drivers they had some spare information-processing capacity in any context and it was their spare capacity that was used in the recognition tasks; but in the busier conditions where the information input from the environment was so much greater, this spare capacity was much reduced.

If more information is available than we are capable of processing then some of it has to be neglected or ignored. The skilled performer knows what information he can afford to ignore. Unfortunately for the adult attempting to learn a new skill the amount of information that reaches him through his sense receptors from the environment may be considerable. He may be quite at a loss to know what aspect of the information is really important and necessary to the decision-making process about what actions to take and what is irrelevant or redundant. Think of the vast quantity of sensory information that reaches a novice driver when he first sits in the driving seat of a car. To begin with he can see the controls, three pedals when he only has two feet, a steering wheel, gear lever, hand brake, ignition key, choke, lighting switches, indicator stem, horn, heater controls and perhaps even a cigarette lighter when he only has two hands. Then there are the numerous dials and lights, all of which have some role to play in the successful driving of the car. As if this visual display was not enough the instructor will go on to explain how to adjust the mirrors so that the driver can see behind as well as in front; explain how to fix and adjust the seat belt and then describe what needs to be done to start the engine.

Once the engine is running the rate of input of information increases considerably. Now there is the sound of the engine and the feel of vibrations through the steering wheel and the seat. The novice's anxiety level will have shot up, he may well have broken out in a cold sweat. The next step, of moving the car, will increase the information input even more. The clutch and accelerator must be balanced just as the instructor describes or else the engine stalls or the car shoots suddenly forward. Assuming our novice begins to drive the car along the road there is new visual information from the approaching bus, the parked car, the dog on the pavement, the child playing ball by the side of the road: all seem important. All the previous information from the car's controls and from the sound of the engine is still there too. It is likely he will be totally overwhelmed by the information reaching him and will panic and stall the engine.

A few months later when he has learned what information to attend to, he will drive smoothly along, anticipate and avoid hazards many yards ahead and will still have enough spare capacity to listen attentively to his car radio. The skilled driver is still provided with the same possible sources of information as impinged upon him when he drove his first few yards. The experienced driver, though, has become more economical in his use of information. He has learned how to obtain the maximum amount of relevant information from the minimum input. How did this change come about?

The Skilled and Unskilled Performance

Let us concentrate first on the ways in which the skilled driver's performance differs from that of the novice driver, for if we are going to understand the processes involved in skill acquisition then we should be able to learn much from considering the differences between the skilled and the unskilled performer and from considering the various transitional stages that the skilled performer passes through as he masters his skill. What we learn from doing this will have relevance for the acquisition of any skill. The driver's task is essentially one of processing information and then making appropriate responses to control a machine. We all have limits to our ability to process information as we have seen. These limits are innate, a consequence of the way the receptors and effectors work and of the structure of the nervous system. In spite of these limits the skilled driver seems able to make so much more of the information that reaches him than does the novice. His performance is smooth and without hesitation, his movements are precise and economical and lead to an accurate pre-determined outcome. The skilled driver has learned how to deal with the information that reaches him in a different way to the novice. He has learned to maximise his ability to handle information connected with the performance of the skill. Put another way, he has learned to overcome to a large extent the limitations of his nervous structure to process information.

If we asked the skilled driver what was going through his mind as he was driving, he would probably describe thoughts largely unconnected with the immediate task in hand. He might describe some thoughts connected with avoiding future hazards, perhaps anticipating the likely traffic conditions at a junction ahead or contemplating the best route for the rest of his journey given it is the rush hour. He would certainly not describe thinking about balancing the movements of the clutch and accelerator pedal to get a smooth gear change or wondering where the hand brake was. The novice driver, however, if he could find the spare capacity to describe his thoughts to us, would be thinking about just such things. For him the demands of the instant are so great that there is no possibility of his planning to avoid the hazards of the future. The immediate demands upon his conscious attention are almost more than he can cope with. Not only does he monitor his own actions in detail as he performs them, watching, for example, as he changes gear, but he is also making an effort to recall the instruction that he has been given. He is talking himself through his activities step by painful step.

The novice driver makes much use of visual feedback from the controls of the car whilst the skilled driver relies to a far greater extent on kinaesthetic information. The experienced driver knows from the feel of his body whether his hands and arms are in the right position to drive the car in a straight line. The novice, on the other hand, must carefully watch the consequences of his actions at the steering wheel to know what effect they will have on the car's path of travel. The experienced driver can tell from the sound of the engine, the feel of the car, and the visual information from the passing world whether the car is in the appropriate gear. He does not need to think about this in his limited conscious attention. The novice, in contrast, having been told that these are the cues that determine the selection of a particular gear will be trying to monitor them with all his attention whilst consciously concentrating on other information relevant to his driving as well.

In isolation our novice driver can almost certainly perform all the sub-routines that go to make up the skill of driving, such as stopping, starting and turning. His instructor will have had him practising them in a quiet side-street where they can be mastered one at a time. On the open road his performance will be awkward. What he lacks at this stage is the ability to organise and co-ordinate these separate sub-routines into a smooth and efficient sequence when he encounters the more demanding environment of a busy road. He is still relying on words to correct and guide his actions because he has not yet acquired an overall plan that relates the sub-routines together. Words are a poor substitute for the fine adjustments that we are capable of making to our physical movements.

In the early stages of the acquisition of any skill our physical movements or motor behaviour are very largely under verbal control. As we practise and become more skilful this need for verbal control and the visual observation of our actions fades; we learn what it feels like to carry out the skilled behaviour effectively. Responses become more and more automatic, needing less and less conscious attention on the learner's part. Practice is essential to the mastering of any skill.

With practice, responses become more and more under internalised control so that attention is freed from the demands of closely monitoring immediate actions and can be used to anticipate and avoid the possible hazards ahead. The novice only has time for the immediate present but the skilled performer has sufficient spare capacity to correct problems before they develop. It is this ability to anticipate hazards which comes with the automatisation of the skill that gives the skilled performer the appearance of being unhurried by comparison with the novice.

The Hierarchical Organisation of Skills

Skills are organised in a hierarchical way, many of the sequences that are carried out by the skilled performer are sub-routines that are repeated time and time again. For example, the sub-routine of changing gear or braking will be carried out many times on a journey. The calling forth of these sub-routines is determined by higher-level programmes which control the overall plan of action. It is the higher-level programme which determines which sub-routines are appropriately called forth. The higher-level programme for our driver may be to drive from home to work and the successful realisation of this overriding plan requires the performance of the appropriate sub-routines of driving to accomplish it. These sub-routines with their hierarchical organisation are the same as the rules (Gagne, 1977) or the plans (Miller, Galanter and Pribram, 1960) that were considered in the last chapter in connection with problem solving. In a really complex skill sub-routines may in their turn involve a series of subordinate sub-routines and so on. Sub-routines do not come ready made, each has had to be learned. The simple act of writing the word 'and' in longhand, for example, once required a conscious plan that governed the nature and order of our individual actions. Indeed this particular sub-routine of writing 'and' has a whole series of sub-sub-routines that in their turn had to be learned. First came mastering holding the pen, then making controlled marks with the pen on paper, and then making the particular marks that represented the letters a, n and d. Later we learned to put the letters together when we mastered the spelling of the word 'and'.

As our level of skill increases, each well-practised set of actions becomes relegated to a lower, more automatic level of control in the overall hierarchy. This gradual increase in the automatisation of responses with practice explains why the proficient actions of the highly skilled operator make comparatively small demands upon his limited capacity to process information. It would seem that in the case of the skilled person it is only the overall plans which occupy his central information-processing capacity, the sub-routines are under automatic control. This obviously implies that when the skilled person is carrying out one of the well-learned automatic sub-routines then he has spare capacity for dealing with other matters in his conscious attention.

Closed-loop and Open-loop Control in Skilled Performance

One suggestion to account for the changes that occur as a person becomes increasingly skilled is that there is a transition from a continuous closed-loop system of control to a situation where there is intermittent open-loop control (Pew, 1966). In a closed-loop system an individual response is made, the feedback or the consequence of the movement is analysed and an appropriate correcting movement is made, the feedback from this response in its turn is analysed and a further correction is initiated. For example, the driver makes a movement of the steering wheel, he observes the consequence of his action in the visual feedback that comes from observing the change in the car's position, further movements are initiated to continue the car in the path required, further monitoring of feedback takes place followed by further correcting movements and so on. This is a closed system: response leads to feedback which leads to new response and further feedback. In an open loop system movements may be made, at least for short periods, without any monitoring of the feedback from the environment. It seems likely that as a person practises his skill and becomes more competent the movement patterns that have been practised become represented centrally in the brain or the spinal cord in some fashion. This programme for controlling the motor side of the skill may be played off rather like a tape or a record without the need for modification from visual, auditory or kinaesthetic feedback, although it is quite possible that this motor programme may be able to detect errors in the motor output via internal feedback (Adams, 1971). As we become more skilled, it seems that we move from a closed-loop system of control to at least a partially open-loop system.

Learning a Skill

Information Necessary for Skill Learning

Let us now look at some of the factors that are important when a person is learning a new skill. To carry out any skilled task a person needs three different kinds of information. First, he must know clearly what he is expected to achieve. This kind of information may be provided externally from plans, instructions, stated objectives or defined standards or it may come from the skilled person himself deciding what his actions are intended to accomplish, as in the case of the artist. Before he starts to master a skill the novice will need to be given a clear impression by his instructor of what kind of performance he is working towards. We could never learn to fly a hang glider unless we were given a clear picture of the skills that we were to master. Demonstration is one of the major ways that the instructor conveys this information about what the novice will be expected to achieve. The demonstration may be augmented by the use of many different kinds of aids.

Secondly, he requires sensory input from the task itself. A person learning a skill needs all the help that he can be given to enable him to discriminate between relevant information from the task, the equipment and the environment and that information which will contribute nothing to the successful performance of the skill. The driving instructor helps the novice discriminate between the relevant cues that signal the appropriate moment for the change of gear and all the other auditory, visual, tactile and kinaesthetic information reaching him. Again demonstration is often used to point up for the novice which informational cues he must attend to.

Thirdly, the learner requires information or feedback about the consequences of his actions. Not only does he need to know what the appropriate response is that should be made at each stage of the skill, he also needs to know whether he has succeeded in making the appropriate response. Feedback is the term that is used to describe the perceptual information that follows as a consequence of the actions taken by a person carrying out a skill. The skilled performer makes use of two different kinds of feedback. Internal feedback is generated, via the kinaesthetic sense receptors in the musles, joints and tendons whenever a physical movement is made. At the same time the action taken creates external feedback. The skilled performer sees his hand move the pen, or hears his voice pitched to the right note. This external feedback comes through the senses of sight, hearing, touch, taste or smell. Often the skilled person's actions generate more information than is needed to guide the action to be taken as the next step in the skill. The person learning a skill needs to be helped to recognise relevant feedback and to ignore any other effects of his actions. The feedback that comes from the changes that are happening in the environment is often known as knowledge of results.

Knowledge of Results and Feedback

Knowledge of results is essential for skill-learning to take place. The skill trainer very often speeds up the process of learning considerably by himself providing the learner with knowledge of results in the early stages of learning. For example, the tennis coach will tell the novice in what ways his service stroke resembles a satisfactory performance. The ball may not land in the area of the court the novice intended, but at least he will know that his racquet grip is correct. Alternatively the trainer may modify or artifically augment in some way the information which comes to the learner about the progress he is making as a result of his actions. The tennis player may be lucky enough to see his attempt at a service played back in slow motion on a video tape-recording.

Thorndike (1927) clearly demonstrated the necessity for knowledge of results in an experiment in which he asked two groups of subjects to draw pencil lines of specified lengths for several days whilst they were blindfolded. One group worked with no knowedge of results and their performance showed no improvement over the period in spite of their considerable practice. The other group was given verbal knowledge of results by the experimenter who told them whether they were right or wrong after each attempt. This group improved considerably.

Knowledge of results is a form of feedback. Miller (1953) has distinguished between two forms in which feedback may be used. He has called these action feedback and learning feedback. Feedback is sometimes used to guide a response once it is under way. For example, the visual feedback that comes from buttering a slice of bread influences how we next move the knife to ensure the butter is evenly spread. This is action feedback. Action feedback provides us with knowlege of the current progress of our attempt to produce results. Feedback may also provide us with information which enables us to improve our next response. For example, observing the consequence of firing one shot may enable us to improve the accuracy of our next shot. This is learning feedback. An important function of the skill trainer is to ensure that the potential learning feedback inherent in a situation is used effectively by the learner as he practises his skill. When we first attempt a new skill much learning feedback may be available to us as a result of our actions but the chances are that unless we are given instruction about what to look for this information will be ignored.

Knowledge of results provides the learner with the information he needs to modify his actions during practice so that his responses may become steadily more accurate. This pattern of learning resembles trial and error learning. Successful responses are more likely to be repeated in the future than unsuccessful ones. This does not mean that the learner needs to be left to master a new skill through a process of trial and error. Indeed, if the skill is at all complex an exclusive reliance on trial and error would be likely to lead to the establishment of a passable but less than efficient or economic performance. Left to practise on a typewriter with no guidance we may become proficient two-finger typists, but we will never learn through trial and error to reach the high speeds of the trained typist. Another of the important functions of the trainer is to give the novice guidance so that as many unnecessary errors as possible may be eliminated at an early stage.

Transfer of Training

Very often when we have mastered a skill we find that we are called upon to exercise it in different contexts or with slightly different kinds of equipment. We may learn to swim in the local swimming pool and then go on to swim in the sea, or perhaps we may master typing on a manual machine and then find that an employer expects us to transfer our skills to an electric typewriter. In both these situations there would be likely to be a fairly high positive transfer of the effects of training in one context on to the performance of the skill in the other. The pool-trained swimmer would cope with waves in the sea, but he would not at first swim as confidently in the sea as he did in the pool. There are, however, situations where negative transfer may occur. If we practise particular responses to specific stimuli then we will have a tendency to produce these responses the next time we find ourselves confronted with the stimuli. If this time different responses are required, then we are likely to become muddled over just how to respond. If we have been driving a car which has the reverse gear position forward to the left then we will be likely to experience negative transfer of training for some time if we find ourselves driving a new car which has the reverse gear back and to the right. Muddles seem most likely to occur when the responses required in the different situations are highly similar but differ in small but important ways. Squash players have some difficulties with negative transfer of training if they take up tennis for although there are many similarities between the two games the skilled squash player uses a wrist action which is unsuitable when hitting a tennis ball. People have considerable problems with negative transfer if they try to learn Spanish and Portuguese at the same time.

The Role of the Skill Trainer

The aim of any successful skill trainer must be to make himself redundant as quickly as possible by enabling the student to evaluate the success of his own performance. The novice must be clear about the criteria by which to judge a successful performance of the skill; he must know where to look for the critical information that will give him the maximum guidance for the performance of his skill and he must know how to evaluate the knowledge of results that follow from his actions. Once he can make accurate assessments in these three areas then the novice is in a position to take over the reinforcing function of the trainer himself. Once a novice can objectively evaluate the quality of his own performance, he beomes able to make improvements to his performance as a result of practice without further external help.

6 SOCIAL LEARNING

Influences on Social Behaviour

Almost all our adult life is spent in social situations where we are involved in interacting with other people. We begin to learn to cope with social relationships from our earliest encounters with our parents and close family and by the time we reach adulthood we have already mastered many social skills. Human social behaviour is extraordinarily complex. Each fresh social encounter is likely to influence our social behaviour in some subtly different way and our actions in their turn will influence others socially.

Social Groups

The range of social settings in which we have to learn to interact with others is very great, ranging from the close intimacy of the family through many different formal and informal groups. Cooley (1909) distinguished between 'primary' and 'secondary' groups and this distinction is still useful. A primary group is one which is small enough for all its members to be involved in face to face interaction and involves the individual fully in mutual identification with the other group members. The family, the peer group of our close friends and sometimes the groups with which we work are all examples in some varying degree of primary groups. A secondary group, by contrast, often involves a contractual association between the members for the achievement of very specific goals. We may never meet many of the other members of a secondary group; those members we do encounter we will relate to in a rather formal and impersonal way and only a small part of our total personality is likely to be involved. A trade union, a professional association or a political organisation are all examples of secondary groups. Each group we find ourselves in, whether primary or secondary, will have expectations about how its members should behave in matters that affect the group. These norms may be formally stated or they may have developed as the result of interaction amongst group members. Whatever their origins, if we disregard these norms we will lay ourselves open to disapproval and possible sanctions by other group members. Some of the groups we join will be of considerable importance to us, such as friendship and work groups; towards others we may have less emotional commitment but none the less modify our behaviour to meet the group norms.

Each group we encounter will have its own structure of power and status; as soon as we become a member we will have a place in the pecking order. In some groups we may have the status or position of leader with considerable power over the management of the group's affairs, in others we may be an insignificant follower with very little power or status. The power of a group member is often related to the control he has over the way ideas and information are communicated within the group. The more central the individual is in the communication structure, the more influence, power and status he usually has.

Closely related to the power and communication structures of the group, is its role structure. Groups usually require a division of labour or function between the group members. Some members will specialise in helping achieve the task for which the group exists, while others may have a role which enables them to contribute more to maintaining the socio-emotional climate of the group. A role represents the behaviour that is expected of the individual depending on his position in the power structure. The roles of group members are interdependent, the role associated with any one position in a group being defined in relationship to the roles of others in related positions. The role of the manager, for example, is defined in terms of the roles of the people he manages. The expectations about the way a person will play a role go beyond simple actions, they also include expectations about motivation, attitudes and values. The roles that we have are specific to particular situations. When we meet a group member outside the group context then we do not normally continue to play our group roles. However, such an encounter may leave us uncertain just how to react. When we meet our boss shopping in the supermarket there may well be an initial awkwardness of reaction.

At any time we will be a member of numerous groups both primary and secondary. Even during the course of a single day we may occupy many different positions in groups and play many different roles from family member, to employee, friend, customer, student and captain of the football team. At many stages of our adult life we will be expected to take on new roles.

The new trainee must play his occupational role quite differently' from that of the senior executive he may one day become. The unattached bachelor at a party can get away with social behaviour which might meet with considerable disapproval amongst the married couples at a playgroup social. At home with our family we are expected to behave differently from at work or at the pub. Each social setting, each new group we join will make different demands on our social behaviour. Even when we reach retirement age we will still find ourselves making changes to our social behaviour to meet the demands of our changed social situation.

Socialisation

All changes to an individual's social behaviour involve learning. The process by which an individual comes to accept the attitudes, values and norms of the social groups of which he is a member is referred to as socialisation. Socialisation begins with the young child who first imitates the behaviour he sees and then, usually, goes on to internalise the values and ideals which underlie the behaviour. In the long term these values and ideals are adopted as the child's own. The process of leading the individual child to an acceptance of the norms of his society is mainly achieved by the face to face groups of which he is a member, such as the family. The socialisation initiated in the family is reinforced and extended by other groups with which he has contact such as the school, the peer group and institutions such as youth groups and clubs. In return for accepting the demands these various groups make upon him the individual receives satisfaction for many of his basic needs.

Our socialisation does not end when we leave school. Each phase of our adult life involves us in learning to play new roles and each phase will extend the process of our socialisation. Consider, for example, the extent of the social learning that faces a young doctor as he makes the transition from medical student to fully qualified general practitioner employed in a group practice. He will already have mastered the medical skills and techniques that will be demanded in his new role and much of the learning we have considered in earlier chapters will be relevant in understanding how this has been acquired. As a student though, he will also have begun to recognise that new forms of social behaviour and new attitudes will be expected of him as a practising doctor both by the other members of his profession and by the public at large.

As a student he will have tried out his new role when dealing with patients in a clinical setting, but if he assumes the norms of his new role too enthusiastically and too soon his fellow students will put him under pressure to revert to the more easy-going, relaxed behaviour they favour as a group. As soon as he becomes a fully qualified professional and joins a group practice he will be expected to identify more fully with his new role. Now he must convey an air of confidence and competence in his dealings with his patients; they will expect him to be formal but approachable. He will receive positive social reinforcement from them for behaviour which fits their stereotype of a doctor. If he appears flustered and in a panic when he encounters an emergency he will soon be made to feel that such behaviour is unacceptable. He will rapidly master what to do, what to say and when. It is likely that his perception of himself will begin to change a little as he becomes more familiar with playing his new role. He will feel social pressure to dress somewhat differently from the way he dressed as a student. These pressures may come rather more from his colleagues than from the majority of his patients. It is possible that to some extent he may model his new behaviour upon that of some doctor he particularly admires. He will probably adopt a subtly different style of speech and modify his way of expressing his thoughts to others, at least when he is dealing with a patient or his professional colleagues. Through these processes of social learning, the new role he has come to play may lead to changes in his very identity as a person.

The socialisation of our doctor into his new role has come about in three different but inter-woven ways. First, there has been an element of operant conditioning; his patients and professional colleagues will have positively reinforced those aspects of his behaviour which they found satisfactory and will have punished through their social disapproval those aspects which they found less acceptable. Secondly, there has been a more overt cognitive element to his socialisation. He will have made a conscious interpretation of the social events in which his new role has involved him. Some changes in his behaviour will have come about through differences in the way he perceives himself. For example, he may well see his informal student dress of sweater and jeans as inappropriate to his new more formal role and hence have taken to wearing a suit and tie. He may have made a conscious effort to respond differently to people with different social backgrounds, probably giving fuller explanations to his middle-class patients. Finally some aspects of his socialisation may have been brought about by his emotional involvement. For instance the emotional pressures that he may have felt when giving comfort to a dying patient and his relatives may well have caused him to feel very intensely the importance of playing his role as the calm, confident professional with total conviction.

These three elements involved in the doctor's socialisation into his new role are in reality interrelated in a very complex fashion. To try to separate them involves making rather arbitrary divisions. In practice, any situation involving new adult social learning is likely to contain some elements of operant conditioning through the application of social rewards and punishment, some element of learning that comes about through changes in the adult's perception and interpretation of social events and some element of learning that has its origins in the adult's emotional involvement.

Affiliation

The many groups of which we have membership during the course of our lives profoundly affect our social learning. Groups enable us to satisfy many of our affiliative needs. Amongst the more obvious reasons for people joining together to form groups is the satisfaction of many of their basic physical and material wants, such as mating, food production and defence against external threats and dangers. We also have a need to feel that we belong together with other people. This need may well have its origins in the operant condition that takes place during those early impressionable years when we are totally dependent for our survival on the family group.

Schachter (1959) examined the relationship between fear and a person's inclination to affiliate with others. All his subjects were told that as part of the experimental procedure they would be given an electric shock; half were warned that this shock would be painful whereas the other half were reassured that they would feel no more than a mere tingle. Questioning after the experiment was over established that the former group had a significantly higher level of fear. Subjects were next told that there would be a delay in the proceedings as it would take ten minutes to set up the apparatus. They were offered the choice of either waiting alone in a comfortable room, or waiting with other subjects in a less comfortable room. Schachter found that whilst about two-thirds of the subjects with a high level of fear choose to wait with others only one-third of the low fear subjects made this choice. When he took into account the subjects' birth position in their families Schachter found that first-born children felt a stronger urge to affiliate under threat than did later-born children. Perhaps the first-born learns to expect greater attention to his fears and anxieties from his family and hence in adult life turns more readily to the support of other people as a means of reducing fear.

Besides reducing fear, affiliation also satisfies a need that we seem to have to compare ourselves socially with others. In many situations we find ourselves in, we have no clear, objective way to establish what forms of behaviour are right or good or acceptable. In such circumstances we look to others around us to provide us with a guide. The norm adopted by the group then becomes our criterion for what seems right. Fashion in clothes can be seen as an obvious example, social comparison providing the norms which guide the individual in his choice of clothes. But looking to see what others are doing before making our own choices may influence our lives much more profoundly. Where we choose to live and work, if, and when and whom we marry, how we bring up our children and even whether we divorce, may all to some extent at least be influenced by making social comparisons between ourselves and others with whom we feel we have much in common. Festinger (1954) has argued that we all have a need to evaluate ourselves, our actions, abilities and opinions and that the way we meet this need is by making social comparisons. Often we are at a loss as to how to behave socially until we have been given a cue by others whose circumstances seem similar to our own.

Values, Attitudes and Opinions

Apart from providing us with guidance on how to behave socially when we are unsure, the groups that we belong to often influence the formation and development of our values, attitudes and opinions. Much of our behaviour will be influenced by the basic underlying values which we acquired during the early years of our socialisation in family and peer group. However, even in the later stages of adult life we may find ourselves modifying our values as the result of the continuing process of socialisation in the groups of which we have membership. We give expression to our values through our attitudes, our opinions and aspects of our overt behaviour. If an individual expresses the opinion that his son should put more effort into his homework he is probably reflecting part of a more general attitude that school work should be taken seriously. This in itself is probably part of a more general value the individual holds that recognises academic achievement as a contributory factor to a person's economic and social standing. The attitudes and values of an individual will relate together to form an attitude system.

Our attitudes have their origins in our past experiences and they very largely determine our future responses to social objects with which they are connected. As such they are rather like a 'set' in problem solving, they give us a particular orientation which spares us the necessity of thinking out our position in relationship to their area of concern each time. When we meet a new person, for example, we look for a number of cues such as appearance, accent, warmth of response and so on in order to place him into a familiar category. Once we have done this we will tend to respond towards him on the basis of the attitudes that we have established in the past to that category of person. As a result of the attitudes we hold, our behaviour becomes more predictable and consistent.

Once we hold an attitude it can affect our perception and interpretation of social situations and objects very markedly. If we hold the attitude that private schools are superior to state schools, then we will tend to notice the evidence that supports our attitude and ignore or undervalue any evidence to the contrary. If, however, the evidence in favour of state education becomes so great that we can no longer ignore it, we will find ourselves in a state of dissonance. Our whole attitude system may find itself under strain and we may only resolve the dissonance or incongruity by restructuring our attitude system.

Even though two people may both hold a positive attitude towards a social object, these attitudes may vary greatly. Attitudes can vary in terms of their direction, whether they are for or against. They can vary in intensity; one person may have a vehement conviction of the importance of private enterprise whilst another merely thinks that on the whole it's no bad thing. They can also vary in terms of their centrality to the whole attitude system of the individual as well as the degree to which they interconnect with other values. One individual's attitude towards emigration may be tied up with his attitudes towards his job prospects, his family and his whole life-style whilst for another emigration may be of very little interest.

Attitudes can be thought of as having three main elements or components: a cognitive component which relates to what we know or believe about the object of the attitude, an affective or emotional component which relates to our feeling about the object of the attitude and a tendency to behave in a particular way in relationship to the object of the attitude. Because attitudes are multi-dimensional they are particularly difficult to measure. Asking someone for their opinion about a social object may tap the cognitive component of an attitude but it may give no indication of the extent of the person's feelings or actions in relationship to the object. We are often very poor predictors of our own behaviour; our statements of intent may be accurate descriptions of our wishes and aspirations but our subsequent behaviour may be quite different and influenced by other factors.

Our attitudes lead to predictability in our behaviour and the smooth functioning of groups depends upon members acting in predictable fashions. It is clear then that there is likely to be a strong pressure exerted by a group upon its members to share attitudes in matters that affect the group. It is very satisfactory and reassuring to find that others are in agreement with our view of things. On the whole people tend to avoid those whose views disagree too markedly with their own. If we value our membership of a particular group then we will be likely to modify our values, attitudes and opinions to conform more with those of other group members. A group that makes us feel a valued and acceptable member does much to boost our self-esteem. When our self-esteem is low we are likely to be most susceptible to group reaction, for then group acceptance will be most rewarding whilst group rejection will lower our self-esteem still further. Groups satisfy very important needs and contribute greatly to our sense of personal identity, but because they are so important to us they can put us under great pressure to conform.

Interpersonal Attraction

In spite of our affiliative needs we do not establish successful social relationships with everyone. There are a number of factors which determine whom we will find socially attractive. Similarity of values, attitudes and interests is an important determinant of who makes friends with whom. Newcomb (1961) in a study of male students sharing a hostel block for 16 weeks found that the similarity of attitudes expressed before the start of the sharing gave a very good indication of who would befriend whom by the end of the period. In some social situations people seem to establish friendship choices with others who complement their own strengths or weaknesses. For example Winch, Ktsanes and Ktsanes (1955) found that with many married couples one partner would complement the other in the way they played their roles. A dominant husband would often have a submissive wife or vice versa. However, what at first may appear to be a friendship choice formed on the basis of complementarity may just be a special instance of similarity, with the couple in complete agreement about how each should play their marriage roles. At this level they can been seen to be sharing a similar attitude about the quality of their relationship.

Before we can learn whether another will be a satisfactory social acquaintance we need to make communication with him, and to do this we must come into some form of contact. Newcomb found that in the early stages of his study physical proximity was a more important determinant of social preference than similarity of attitudes. Festinger *et al.* (1950) investigated friendship choices amongst 270 families living in a relatively self-contained and isolated student housing project. The investigators found that the farther people lived from each other, the less they saw of each other socially. They also found that people who used the same stairways and utility rooms mixed more socially than did people who used different ones even though their flats might be close together.

Exchange Theory

We have seen that there is often an element of operant conditioning at work in social interactions. Some people seem to provide us with more of the rewards and reinforcements that we want than others. Homans (1958) and Thibaut and Kelley (1959) have suggested that we can look on social behaviour in terms of the costs and benefits rather as though social behaviour involved the exchange of goods. In exchange theory the rewards we may get from a social encounter may relate to the satisfaction of our primary needs for food, drink and so on or to our need for secondary social reinforcers such as approval or enhanced prestige. The costs to us may include fatigue, boredom, increased anxiety, fear, embarrassment or the loss of prestige or reputation. According to Homans' view a person will maintain social interaction with another if the profit from it is enough to satisfy the expectations he has developed as the result of previous experiences, and if it promises to be more profitable than any alternative social interaction that is available. The profitability of a social interaction is not measured simply in terms of its rewards, but in terms of the excess of profit over the costs which the interaction will incur. We may reject a relationship which offers high rewards at great cost in favour of a relationship which is less rewarding but more profitable because it involves a far lower cost. Exchange theory indicates the ways in which the relationships between people can be maintained, strengthened, or extinguished through the effects of operant conditioning.

Group Structures and Processes

Let us now look in more detail at some of the structures and processes that characterise groups. When a group comes into being it involves some kind of interaction amongst its members; from this interaction a relatively stable pattern of relationships between the group members develops with some agreement about common goals. There will be a certain level of cohesiveness amongst the group members and a set of norms and structures will evolve.

Some groups are formal and will have explicitly stated goals which are accepted by all members of the group. Such would be the case, for example with an operatic society, an evening class or a research and development team in a factory. Even formal groups with varied specific goals may well satisfy a range of different needs amongst the group members. The people coming together to sing, study or work on a specific task will interact socially. Besides the satisfactions that will come from helping the group realise its goals, individual members may well satisfy their need to participate, or for recognition or prestige. Other groups are more informal and may allow their members to pursue a series of short-term goals whilst providing a milieu in which they can satisfy their personal needs for friendship and a sense of belonging. Such an informal group of friends may meet to play bridge together on one occasion, next organise a theatre trip and then spend a day walking together in the country.

Group Cohesion

Not all groups are equally attractive to their members. Some groups have a greater degree of unity or cohesiveness amongst the group members than others. Highly cohesive groups seem to have all or some of the following characteristics. There is a high level of mutual attraction amongst the group members. This does not necessarily mean that all the members personally like each other but that they do get reward or satsifaction from interacting together. The members of cohesive groups share attitudes, particularly in connection with matters that relate to the group and there exists a well developed and accepted structure to the group. Members know where they stand in relationship to each other and are clear about the roles they are personally expected to play within the group. In a highly cohesive group there will be strong conformity to the group's norms; there is likely to be a stable and long-lasting membership and a low level of absenteeism from group activities. Group cohesiveness increases when the group perceives itself under attack in some way from outside forces. For example, the parent-teacher association which has had an indifferent history may suddenly find a new vigour and dynamism when the local education authority threatens to close the school.

Group Norms

As soon as people interact together for any length of time expectations about one another's patterns of behaviour will develop; it is these expectations which constitute the norms of the group. The existence of norms enables the group to function smoothly because the group members can make accurate predictions about each other's behaviour in matters which affect the smooth running and well-being of the group. Groups can only run smoothly when the norms are observed. No group can ever hope to meet the needs of its members completely all the time. On occasions there is likely to be a conflict between the needs of the individual and the behaviour demanded by the group. Schachter (1951) has shown that when a member deviates from the norms of his group the other members at first increase their rate of communication with him in order to try and persuade him to fall back into line. If this increased attention fails and it becomes clear that the individual is not prepared to conform to the group norms then he will be ignored and rejected by the group. At this point the deviate is likely to give up his group membership.

Some norms are less central to a group's well-being than others. A member who misses the occasional practice will cause less consternation to his fellows in a choir than the member who persistently sings out of tune. Deviance from central norms causes most threat to a group. The extent to which a member may safely deviate from more peripheral norms depends to a large extent upon his status within the group. A leader can deviate from peripheral norms, presumably because his acceptance of the central norms is never open to doubt, whereas a newcomer to a group, whose loyalty is less certain, is expected to conform more strictly to all the group norms. For example, the leader of a religious group may question some aspects of accepted dogma whilst the new convert will adhere firmly to every fine point, at least until the sincerity of his conversion is beyond question.

Reference Groups

When we identify with the goals and norms of a group and adopt the values and attitudes of its members it becomes for us a reference group. It is not essential to be a member of a group for it to act as a reference group. Adolescents in particular often absorb the norms and attitudes, at least as they imagine them to be, of groups that they would like to join. Sometimes we may find ourselves forced into membership of a group by circumstances beyond our control but if we are not happy with its norms and attitudes then it will not act as a reference group. Such might be the case of the holiday-maker who finds he has to cope with uncongenial fellow travellers on a tour.Such a group may become a negative reference group with the individual deliberately reacting in opposition to the norms of the majority. On other occasions we may find ourselves in a conflict because we owe allegiance to two groups which have incompatible norms in some areas. Such is often the case for the foreman in industry. He owes some allegiance to the management group and some to the work group with whom he is involved. He is forced into the position of a 'marginal man', unable to reject or fully join either group.

Each individual is involved in his own system of overlapping social groupings and each group in some way will influence his loyalties, his expectations and his perspectives. Almost all formal adult learning takes place in social settings of one kind or another. The adult's experiences in other groups will be likely to have some influence upon the way in which he engages in this learning.

7 PERSONALITY DIFFERENCES AND COGNITIVE STYLE

Individual Differences

So far in this book, when adult learning has been under discussion we have concentrated upon the similarities between people. In this way it has been possible to identify some of the general rules about the basic processes of learning. All people (except for a very few with obvious defects), are born with the same mechanisms for learning to comprehend, make predictions about and take action in the world around them. In spite of the similarity in our basic physiology, the diversity of human behaviour is enormous. By the time we reach adulthood we have all acquired different interests, knowledge, aptitudes, skills, attitudes and motivations. As a result of these differences we are each drawn to learn different things at different times and with differing degrees of facility and personal involvement. In this chapter and the next, we will explore some of these individual differences and consider their possible implications for the way that people learn.

Although there is great diversity amongst people, most individuals are remarkably consistent over long periods of time in the way that they think, experience their environment and behave towards it. These relatively stable ways of responding towards the world are all manifestations of the individual's personality. The task of attempting to describe and define personality is very complex; in this book we do not have space to do more than examine briefly some of those aspects of personality which appear to influence the style and effectiveness of the individual's learning.

Intelligence

Intelligence is often regarded as the most significant difference between individuals when it comes to considering factors which may influence individual learning. That differences in the distribution of human abilities exist seems self evident. Unfortunately, when we attempt to measure what these differences are for any individual adult we soon find ourselves in difficulties. Most of the literature on the definition and assessment of intelligence derives from work that has its origins in attempts to identify as accurately as possible individual children's actual and potential ability to learn, reason and solve

98

problems. Although intelligence is a concept which is widely used it still escapes precise definition. There are so many forms of behaviour indicative of intelligence that to get to the essence of intelligence seems an almost impossible task. At the moment there is no completely satisfactory test or procedure for predicting an adult's potential ability to learn. Very few existing intelligence test items correspond to the kind of competencies that adults set out to acquire. The most widely used test of adult intelligence is the Wechsler Adult Intelligence Scale (Wechsler, 1958). This scale has eleven sub-tests which sample a number of mental activities such as vocabulary, general knowledge, common sense, arithmetic ability and short-term memory, speed of mental functioning and the ability to relate one thing to another logically. The scores obtained by using the WAIS provide a general estimate of the limits of the individual's performance on mental tasks. Scores obtained from the WAIS do give a useful estimate of the way an adult will perform on verbal learning tasks in educational settings (Knox, Grotelueschen and Sjorgren, 1968). They provide a less realistic estimate of how effectively the individual will learn to programme a computer, manage an office, or operate a machine tool.

The way in which an adult tackles new learning tasks is a product of both innate ability and accumulated experience. D.O. Hebb (1949) helped to identify the problems that face anyone attempting to measure intelligent behaviour when he distinguished between two measures of intelligence which he called Intelligence A and Intelligence B. Intelligence A is the innate potential which we acquire from our genetic make-up and which will manifest itself in a good brain and a good neural metabolism. Intelligence A sets the limits to the individual's capacity to develop intelligent responses. Intelligence B is the level of functioning of a particular brain after development has gone on, it is the result of an interaction between Intelligence A and a particular environment. No environment is ever totally ideal so it is unlikely that an individual's full potential will ever be fully realised. Intelligence B will always be less than Intelligence A. However, neither A nor B can be directly measured. Intelligence A will always be masked by the effects of environmental experience and Intelligence B may grow and develop dependent upon the environmental experiences of the individual. To measure Intelligence B adequately we would need to observe all the intelligent acts of the individual from birth to death. The best we can do in reality is to take a sample of Intelligence B. P.E. Vernon (1955) has suggested that we could usefully use the term Intelligence C to describe the sample of Intelligence B that is obtained using a standardised test of intelligence.

It is Intelligence A that the educationalist would like to measure so as to provide the optimum environment to develop Intelligence B. The closest measure he can get is Intelligence C. By the time an individual reaches adulthood his environmental experiences will have contributed much to his intellectual performance; to get a representative sample of an adult's Intelligence B any test of adult intelligence would need to take full account of this.

Research using the intelligence tests which are available to measure adult intelligence indicate that there is a high degree of stability in an individual's test scores at least between the ages of 20 and 50 and even beyond (Cunningham and Birren, 1976; Green, 1969). Many of these studies have been longitudinal, that is to say, the same subjects have been tested using the same intelligence test on a number of occasions over the years. Most of these longitudinal studies of adult intelligence have been with subjects who had experience of higher education either at college or university. The general finding is that the more able the subject, as measured by the tests, the more rapidly he tends to learn and the more readily he copes with complex tasks. In contrast with the general adult population, the more able subjects had a greater tendency to increase their test scores over time, or at least to remain stable (Bayley and Oden, 1955; Blum and Jarvik, 1974). Other research based on studies of a cross-section of disparately aged subjects all tested at the same time seems to suggest that the range of individual differences in intelligence increases with age. The more intellectually able show a more rapid increase in their measured intelligence during childhood and adolescence and then seem to reach a higher plateau in young adulthood; they then maintain or even gradually increase their scores as they grow older. The less intelligent, as measured by the tests, increase their scores more slowly, reach a much lower plateau at an earlier age and then go into a decline as they age. As a result of the changes with age there seems to be a greater range of intelligence in a representative group of 50-year-olds than in a similar group of 20-year-olds (Foulds and Raven, 1948; Foulds, 1949; Roberts, 1968). Although there is some stability in intelligence test scores over time, this does not necessarily mean that there is no qualitative change in adult intelligence with age.

There is much debate about the structure of the intellect (Butcher, 1968). One attempt to identify our primary mental abilities by analysing the factors which contribute to intelligence test scores has suggested that these scores are, at least in part, the product of two contrasting but interacting types of intelligence. These have been called fluid intelligence and crystallised intelligence (Cattell, 1963). They have much in common with Hebb's Intelligence A and Intelligence B. Fluid intelligence is rather formless and is relatively independent of education and experience and it can flow into a wide range of intellectual activities. It is involved in our ability to perceive complex relationships, to recognise and retain an awareness of the immediate environment as in short-term memory, to form concepts and to engage in abstract reasoning. The basis of our fluid intelligence is our neurophysiological structure which depends partly on our heredity, but can also be influenced by such factors as injury or disease.

Crystallised intelligence is the result of fluid intelligence being mixed with cultural knowledge. It is crystallised because it is a precipitate out of experience. It increases with the individual's experience of life and formal education both of which provide him with ways and means of dealing with his new experiences. The sorts of abilities that demonstrate crystallised intelligence include general information, verbal comprehension, coping with social situations and arithmetic reasoning.

Interacting together these two kinds of intelligence are involved in many of the learning tasks that adults undertake. They can be complementary for in some learning tasks either crystallised or fluid intelligence may be called upon. One subject may solve a problem using fluid intelligence to discover a brilliant and original solution, another may solve the same problem by applying his accumulated experience.

Both fluid and crystallised intelligence develop during childhood and adolescence. However, as the neurological structures reach full maturity and then begin to suffer damage as the result of injury, disease and so on during adulthood, there is a decrease in fluid intelligence. For most of us, it is suggested, fluid intelligence has begun to decline before we are out of our twenties. However, on a happier note, the evidence suggests that crystallised intelligence increases, albeit gradually, during much of adulthood. The older person compensates for the decrement in fluid intelligence by drawing upon his crystallised intelligence. He relies on wisdom in place of sheer brilliance!

It is perhaps significant that the greatest intellectual productivity tends to occur when people are in their thirties or early forties whilst the most significant creative work, at least in many areas, is carried out by younger people. Most adults in their forties and fifties have an ability to learn comparable to that they possessed when in their twenties, if they are in a position to control the pace of their learning. However, learning tasks that are paced, complex or place a heavy load on short-term memory are more likely to suffer as we grow older. Most intelligence tests measure both fluid and crystallised intelligence. Crystallised intelligence is largely influenced by the extent to which the individual continues to seek information and engage in educational activity. This perhaps accounts for the finding that the better educated show less decline in intelligence test scores with ageing.

Personality

The study of personality has long been a major concern of psychology, none the less the task of attempting to describe and define the extraordinary complexity of the interactions between a person's character, temperament, intelligence, and physiology which result in that more or less stable way of approaching the environment that we recognise as personality, has proved very difficult. Many different models for the description of personality have been advanced (Hall and Lindzey, 1970) and it is quite beyond the scope of this chapter to describe or evaluate their usefulness. There are, however, a number of personality characteristics which research has shown influence the use we make of our intellectual potential and we will now turn our attention to these.

Many descriptions of aspects of personality assume that the individual can be placed somewhere upon a continuum that extends between the extremes of a pair of alternatives. Different theorists favour different dimensions as necessary to give an adequate description of personality. We will consider a number of the dimensions that theorists have advanced which have been found to have a bearing upon the way in which the individual approaches learning tasks.

Eysenck (1960) has suggested that there are two major dimensions needed to express the main characteristics of the personality. His model of the personality has one continuum stretching between the extremes of introversion and extraversion and a second continuum between neuroticism and stability. The typical introvert is a quiet, rather shy and private person. He prefers books to people. He likes to plan things ahead. He has his emotions under fairly tight control. Life for him is a serious affair and he tends to take a rather pessimistic view. He is reliable in his dealings with others and sets himself high ethical standards. The typical extravert, on the other hand, is very sociable and outgoing. He prefers not to study, at least not by himself. He is impulsive and tends to do things on the spur of the moment. He likes plenty of action in his world. His emotions are often given free play. He will, for example, quickly lose his temper with others. He is not especially reliable. The extreme neurotic is often anxious and feels generally nervous and insecure. He is unsure of himself and worried about what the world may spring on him next. The stable individual is calm and relaxed about things, he has the conviction that basically he can cope with life and he will not be easily ruffled. According to Eysenck an individual's position on one dimension is quite unrelated to his position on the other.

Eysenck (1967) has suggested that there are physiological differences which underlie the introversion-extraversion dimension. Extraverts have higher arousal thresholds than introverts in the brain stem reticular system, this leads to a lower level of arousal in the cortex of the brain. It takes more input from the environment to make an impact on the nervous system of the extravert. In order to achieve an optimum level of arousal the extravert seeks out extra stimulation. As a result of these basic differences introverts and extraverts come to respond differently to the world around them. The introvert, for example, is more readily classically conditioned than the extravert (Eysenck, 1957). One consequence of this is that the introvert tends to have more of a guilty conscience when he breaks rules. He is often rather over-socialised whilst the extravert, who is more difficult to condition, is relatively under-socialised and hence he is more likely to kick over the traces. Besides the strength of conscience, which may clearly influence a learner's feelings about sticking to his studies, Shadbolt and Leith (1967) have shown that personality differences may influence which method of teaching is most successful with an individual. They presented two different forms of a programmed text to some 200 college of education students. One form was highly structured, the other version required a much greater tolerance of uncertainty in looking for explanatory principles. Introverts did best with the clearly structured, well guided programme whilst extraverts did not do well with this form. They were more successful than the introverts, however, with the programme that required them to work things out for themselves. Introverts seem to prefer to have a clear view of the logical structure of the material they are to learn. Extraverts on the other hand seem to find little help from the structure immediately and prefer to explore the material and to work a structure out for themselves. Overall the more stable subjects were more successful than the neurotics were. In another study with 40-year-olds in which different methods of giving training in the decimal currency system were investigated, Leith *et al.* (1968) again found a preference by extraverts for unstructured teaching materials.

Howarth and Eysenck (1968) showed that there was a difference between introverts and extraverts in learning to associate word pairs Subjects were selected as having high scores on the introversion-extraversion dimension. All subjects had to learn seven word pairs and were then tested at five different recall intervals ranging from a few minutes to 24 hours. The results showed that extraverts did best when they were asked to recall the material within 5 minutes of their learning it whereas the introverts remembered more when the period before recall was longer.

A study by Huckabee (1974) suggests that there is a relationship between extraversion and the form in which material may be held in memory. The 111 students enrolled on a psychology course rated the ease with which a series of abstract and concrete nouns aroused a mental picture. When ratings were compared with extraversion scores it was found that the introverts had high imagery scores. This tendency was stronger for concrete rather than abstract nouns. It would seem very likely that introverts may more readily store their memories in visual form whereas extraverts may favour verbal storage.

Cognitive Style

Convergent and Divergent Thinking

Guilford (1956) introduced a model of the structure of the intellect in which he differentiated between a number of cognitive operations including convergent thinking and divergent thinking. In convergent thinking operations the information leads either to one right answer or at least to an answer which is recognised as the best or the conventional one. Conventional intelligence test items typically require convergent answers. For example, there is only one obvious answer that will complete the sequence A, C, F, J, -. The 'right' answer is O. However, in divergent thinking we think in different directions; there is no 'right' answer but often many equally acceptable solutions. The quality of divergent thought is judged in terms of the quantity, variety and originality of the responses. A request to think of as many uses as possible for a hip-bath would require divergent thinking, plainly there is no one right answer. Divergent thought soon became equated with creativity although it is now clear that there is far more to creativity than a high level of divergent thought (MacKinnon,

1962). Guilford initially suggested that divergent thinking and intelligence were distinct. Subsequent evidence (Yamamoto, 1965; Ginsburg and Whittlemore, 1968) is less clear-cut. It appears that intelligence test scores and divergence test scores are related for low and moderate levels of intelligence but with high levels of intelligence the relationship between the test scores becomes increasingly random.

Hudson (1966) investigated the possible connection between convergent and divergent thought and the subject choices that adolescents made when they entered a grammar school sixth form. He found that science students, especially those specialising in physics, tended to prefer a convergent style of thought whilst arts students were more likely to be divergent thinkers, particularly those studying English literature, history and modern languages. Later work (Hudson, 1968) has suggested that the tests of divergent thought are less a measure of creativity than a sampling of the individual's preferred style of thought. Hudson found that the typical converger had a view of himself as basically cold, dull, and unimaginative whereas the diverger saw himself as warm, imaginative and exciting but at the same time somewhat lacking in manliness and dependability. Each appeared to adopt the style of thought that fitted his self-image. It would seem that mature adults will be subject to much the same processes as Hudson's sixth formers; if this is indeed the case then we might expect certain areas of study or work to attract particular individuals because they identify themselves with the conventional image associated with that area. For example, sixth formers saw physicists as dependable, hardworking, manly and valuable whereas a novelist was seen as imaginative, warm and exciting as a person.

Syllabus-bound and Syllabus-free Learners

Another useful bipolar dimension that has emerged is known as the syllabus-bound and syllabus-free orientation. Hudson (1968) used the abbreviations 'sylb' and 'sylf' to describe the contrasting styles. He found a relationship between 'sylbs' and convergent thinkers and 'sylfs' and divergent thinkers. The typical 'sylb' is almost exclusively concerned with getting good examination marks and happily accepts the restrictions of the formal syllabus. The 'sylf' on the other hand has intellectual interests that extend far beyond the syllabus, very often he has difficulty in confining his study to the narrow requirements of the syllabus. Parlett (1969) found that 'sylbs' were exam-oriented and had few strong personal interests and commitments in connection with their academic work. He found that 'sylbs' on university courses attended more lectures, did more work at home, were more likely to chose a seat at the front of the class and had higher marks in exams. When it came to individual project work 'sylbs' tended to be less successful than 'sylfs'. Parlett came to the conclusion that whilst the conventionally organised system of academic teaching suited 'sylb' students admirably, the 'sylfs' were less satisfied and could have been more successful if they could have had the freedom to organise their academic study to suit their personal curiosity and interests. In one study Josephs and Smithers (1975) gave a battery of tests to 218 upper sixth formers; they identified the 'sylbs' as more conservative, controlled, conscientious and persistent, shy, cautious and practical when contrasted with the 'sylfs'. They were also somewhat more sober, apprehensive and dependent upon their group. They also conformed to the major characteristics of the dogmatic person as identified by Rokeach (1960); they had an authoritarian outlook on life which involved a relatively closed way of thinking and an intolerance towards others whose views differed from their own. It is obvious that a 'sylb' and a 'sylf' would approach their learning in radically different ways and that they would be likely to respond very differently to the approaches of a teacher or instructor depending upon whether his style of teaching was essentially syllabus-bound or syllabus-free.

Serialist and Holist Approaches to Learning

Pask (1969) has distinguished between two major categories of mental competence which reflect the individual's cognitive style and which lead him, in a situation where he has a choice, to prefer one kind of learning strategy to another. He has called the individuals fitting the two major categories 'serialists' and 'holists'. The serialist approaches the study of new material by stringing a sequence of cognitive structures together. The typical serialist will assimilate lengthy sequences of information in this way and as a result is very intolerant of redundant information because of the extra burden it imposes on memory. The holist in contrast learns, remembers and recalls material as a whole. The serialist will prefer to build up a total picture by stringing the detail together. The holist's approach on the other hand is to attempt to gain an overview of an area of study so that the detail can fall into place. The holist has a high order of relations between the details he is learning whilst the serialist has a low order of relations.

Field-dependence, Field-independence and Learning

Witkin *et al.* (1954) found that people differ from each other in the characteristic ways in which they perceive both the environment and themselves in relationship to it. A subject sitting in a chair, which may or may not be fully upright, has two major cues about his orientation, visual information from the chair and the external surroundings and internal, proprioceptive information about body position largely from muscle tension and from the vestibular system in the ear. If both the room and the chair are tipped to the same degree, the only source of information the subject then has is from his internal, proprioceptive sense receptors. Witkin found that some people tended to rely entirely on external cues; as they were influenced by information from the outside world he called them field-dependent. Others relied exclusively on their own interal sensory processes, and were unswayed by contradictory external evidence, these he called field-independent. Most people are not at the extremes of either category, but individuals do tend, over a period of time, to be stable in the degree to which they are field-dependent or field-independent.

Witkin (1969) has gone on to argue that these perceptual characteristics are related to aspects of intellectual behaviour. Field-dependent subjects require work that involves them with people whilst the field-independent individual will work quite successfully alone. Field-independent subjects tend to be more analytical in their thought, to have higher scores on spatial tasks and to perform well in mathematics and scientific subjects.

Impulsivity and Reflectivity

Kagan (1965) working with children has shown that when faced with a problem solving task some children will impulsively blurt out the first possible solution that occurs to them and that this answer is frequently incorrect. Other children, however, are much more reflective. They delay a long time before venturing a solution and are usually correct. This dimension of impulsivity-reflectivity seems to be attitudinal in its origin and it generalises into many learning situations where ideas need to be evaluated. The reflective subject seems to have a strong desire to be right first time and can tolerate the subtle psychological pressures that can be created by the long pause he often needs during which each alternative hypothesis is evaluated in his mind. The impulsive learner by contrast tends to rely on the teacher or some external source for the evaluation of his solutions. He blurts them out in rapid succession quite uncritically and waits for an external hint that he has hit the mark. As children grow older they tend to become more reflective in their approach to cognitive tasks. None the less there are many adult learners who do themselves less than justice because they respond impulsively and will not take the necessary time to evaluate their own solution.

Individual Differences and Adult Learning

We have considered research into a wide range of factors that may influence the way the individual approaches his learning. In time it is probable that some of the dimensions will be shown to be interrelated and perhaps to have a common underlying cause. From a practical point of view it is important to remember that very few people will be at the extreme positions on the dimensions we have considered. For most learners each of the dimensions we have explored may have some bearing upon the way that they approach their learning. When an adult encounters a learning situation that suits his preferred learning style he is likely to learn more from it than if his personal predilections are ignored. For some people who approach the extremes of the dimensions we have considered, their personality characteristics may significantly inhibit their ability to learn in certain settings. For teachers there is an implied warning here: the style of teaching they prefer may well not suit all learners equally. As learners we may find that one approach to study suits us far better than another.

8 INDIVIDUAL DIFFERENCES IN AGE, EXPERIENCE, MOTIVATION AND SELF-PERCEPTION

Influences on the Willingness to Learn

Individuals differ in their motivation to learn. One person, at the age of 30, may give up what to many would seem a successful career and at considerable material sacrifice go off to university for three years to read for a degree, another may go out regularly two evenings every week after a gruelling day's work in order to study a language at an evening class. A third person may be reluctant to attend a short course to train for a new career even though his skill is no longer in demand and he has been unemployed for three years. Individual differences in motivation are plainly a very potent influence upon adult learning. In this chapter we will examine some of the factors which influence the individual's willingness to undertake new learning.

Motivation

Motivation is the process which leads the individual to attempt to satisfy some need. The simplest model of the relationship between motivation and learning assumes that, when a need exists, it will lead to a drive which energises behaviour so that the individual will engage in some appropriate activity in an attempt to satisfy the need. If this activity does lead to a reduction in the drive then the activity will be reinforced or strengthened so that it will be more likely to occur on future occasions. The reinforcement that results from the drive reduction causes learning to take place. This is the law of effect in operation.

In some instances the need which leads to learning may be easy to recognise and have its origins in biological processes such as hunger or thirst; in other instances the need may be much more complex and have its origin in social processes and the view which the individual has of himself as a person. It would be impossible to describe in biological terms the needs which might motivate a 30-year-old to change the whole course of his life by leaving a well-established career to attend university. However, if we were to learn something of the way this person viewed himself we might find that he considered his existing career as something that he had drifted into; it had never stretched him intellectually to any extent. To the casual observer his career may seem challenging and worthwhile, but because he has never felt a sense of personal attainment in succeeding in this area he finds little value in his achievement. He may well have an image of himself as someone who could have succeeded academically. It may be the need to prove to himself that this image is a realistic one, to increase his self-esteem in his own eyes, that has spurred him on to make the apparently irrational sacrifices that will be necessary to attend university.

Maslow (1943) has advanced a theory of human motivation which is helpful in understanding the complexity of motives which are probably at work in such a case as the one we have just been considering. He distinguishes five basic needs which are related to one another in a hierarchy. These needs, according to Maslow, are first for physiological satisfaction, then for safety, love, esteem and self-actualisation. We are also motivated by the desire to bring about or maintain the appropriate conditions which will allow us to satisfy these basic needs. Maslow also adds a sixth need, for knowledge and understanding but he does not relate this directly to the hierarchy of basic needs.

The physiological needs arise from a homeostatic imbalance in the body's automatic regulatory system. The body has a need for oxygen, for food and for water. If any of these physiological needs are unsatisfied then they will dominate consciousness and cause the individual to organise his resources to obtain them. The higher order needs will be forgotten or minimised until this most basic need has been satisfield. Keys (1952) has shown how 26 men kept on a semi-starvation diet for a period of six months but otherwise able to lead a normal life soon became preoccupied almost exclusively with food. Their intense interest in food made it almost impossible for them to concentrate on the tasks they had decided to work on. If they tried to study they found themselves day-dreaming about food. Their feelings altered, they became generally dejected and were quickly irritated by one another's mannerisms. They became far less sociable and developed very negative attitudes to strangers, particularly to strangers who claimed to know what it felt like to go hungry. Once a need has been satisfied, however, it ceases to be an active motivator. Instead the next need in the hierarchy will emerge and in its turn dominate the consciousness and act as the focus for the organisation of the individual's behaviour.

Once the organic needs are satisfied, the safety needs come to the fore. The normal member of our society prefers to have a safe, orderly, predictable, organised world that he can be confident will not suddenly become unmanageable or dangerous. Most adults living in a well-ordered society do not have safety needs as active motivators although Maslow does suggest that our preference for the familiar over the unfamiliar and our tendency to organise the world through philosophy, religion or science, in order to increase its coherence and meaningfulness, is at least in part motivated by our safety needs.

When both the lower order needs are fairly well gratified the need for love, affection and belongingness will emerge. The individual will want friends, a partner, children. He will feel a need for the affiliation with people in groups which we saw was such a potent influence on social learning.

Everyone has a need to be able to hold themselves in high self-esteem and to feel that they are appropriately esteemed by others. The basis of this esteem must be firmly based on real achievement and worth. Maslow sees two subsidiary esteem needs. The first is the desire to have confidence in oneself as the result of personal adequacy and achievement; the second is the desire for reputation, prestige and appreciation from others. When the individual is able to satisfy his self-esteem needs, it leads him to a feeling of self-confidence, worth and capability; a feeling of being a useful and necessary person. When these needs are thwarted the individual will feel weak, helpless and inferior.

At the top of the hierarchy Maslow places the need for self-actualisation; the need to fulfil one's potentialities. 'A musician must make music, an artist must paint, a poet write if he is to be ultimately happy. What a man can be, he must be,' maintains Maslow (1943). Effective self-actualisation depends on being able to recognise one's own capabilities, on being able to recognise what one is capable of becoming. It is the rare individual who reaches a full state of self-actualisation and becomes able to accept and depend upon the self rather than identifying with others, who becomes able to rely on his own standards and to detach himself from customs and social demands when necessary.

Maslow also suggests that largely independent of the hierarchy of needs there are motivational tendencies to obtain knowledge and understanding. Knowledge and understanding may contribute to the attainment of the range of needs, for example, knowledge may help in making sure one's world is safe or in another way may contribute to achieving self-actualisation. Apart from this Maslow has found evidence from his clinical work of a basic need first to know and then to come to understand, systemise, organise, analyse and to see the world as meaningful. Often the satisfaction of these higher order needs goes with the desire to satisfy aesthetic needs (Maslow, 1968).

Although our needs start at a physiological level what becomes clear from a consideration of Maslow's hierarchy is that the higher order needs are closely related to the individual's self-concept. Later in the chapter we will consider the origins of the self-concept and note in particular the contribution made to it by other people; but first we will consider some other needs that seem very relevant to adult learning.

The Need for Stimulation

The human brain is built to be active; it seems to require stimulation from the environment to maintain its optimum level of functioning. It is perhaps because of this that we seem to have an almost insatiable interest in exploring our environment and manipulating the objects in it. Berlyne (1960) has shown that incongruity, complexity, elements of surprise and irregularity are characteristics of visual material which will arouse curiosity in a person so that he will be motivated to spend longer looking at it. Individuals will often engage in activities which could be regarded as work in some circumstances simply for the pleasure of manipulating objects or ideas, or of solving problems. The need to explore manifests itself in such activities as the desire to read, to listen to music, to find out about scientific advances, to study painting or sculpture, to learn about the workings of machines and equipment, to see the latest play or film. Individuals frequently seek out unnecessary intellectual activity in one form or another, such as trying to solve cross-word puzzles or playing games of strategy such as chess or bridge.

When an individual is deprived of his normal amount of stimulation he becomes increasingly unhappy. Bexton, Heron and Scott (1954) paid college students a handsome daily fee of $20 for the tedious task of lying on a bed in a small sound-deadened room for twenty-four hours a day (with time out for meals). The stimulation in the room was kept to an absolute minimum. The subjects wore translucent goggles to minimise visual stimulation and gloves and cuffs to reduce tactile stimulation. The subjects were well motivated for perhaps four to eight hours and then became increasingly bored, restless and irritable. They began to invent ways to stimulate themselves such as touching their fingers together or jerking their muscles. They eagerly requested to hear, time and time again, a recording of an old stock market report. After a day or two in this state of sensory deprivation many of the subjects began to experience hallucinations which became more complex as time went on. The subjects seemed to be producing their own sensory stimulation to compensate for its lack in the environment. Man is an active, experience-seeking animal who is unlikely to be deflected from learning simply because it involves hard work.

Differences in Achievement Motivation

On the other hand, as we saw at the beginning of the chapter, adults do manifestly differ in their responses to learning oppoi tunities. Some people strive against considerable odds to seek out opportunities for new learning whilst others will avoid the opportunity to learn even when it is to their obvious advantage and few barriers stand in their way. Once they are engaged in learning some people will approach it with great enthusiasm and commitment whilst others may just idle along with little evidence of personal involvement.

The reasons for these differences in motivation are very complex. In some instances it may be due to an antipathy of the individual for any educational undertaking which has its origins in schoolday experiences and the early influence of home and neighbourhood upon attitudes towards education. In other cases it may be due to some of the personality factors we explored in the past chapter. Sometimes an individual who is indifferent to learning in a formal setting will devour new ideas and information that relate to some enthusiasm in his everday life such as music or horse-racing. Some social psychologists have drawn particular attention to the influence of child rearing practices upon the need which the individual has to achieve — to do well in relation to some standard of excellence. The study of achievement motivation has its origin in the work of McClelland (McClelland *et al.*, 1953). It has typically been assessed by the use of projective tests in which subjects have been asked to write short stories in response to pictures. Individuals scoring high on achievement motivation show a greater preference for moderately difficult tasks, prefer to take moderate risks in tasks involving skill and ability, have a greater level of self-confidence and are more prepared to put off the possibility of immediate rewards in order to obtain a later gratification. Evans (1967) has shown that students high in achievement motivation were prepared to spend more time on a learning task and were better at it.

The origins of a high level of achievement motivation are to be found in childhood. Winterbottom (1953) found that children who score highly come from families where the mother was concerned with early independence training. The children were expected to take the lead with others, to be self assertive, to make their own friends and to attempt difficult tasks without help. The mothers were more likely to use physical expressions of affection like hugging and kissing. The children with low achievement motivation scores had mothers who believed in routine compliance and who put more restrictions on behaviour. These mothers were also more indulgent with their children and prepared to accept lower standards of work. What this study showed is that achievement motivation is socially determined; some mothers define the way they expect their children to play their roles in such a way that the children come to value achievement. When they reach adulthood such children will be likely to choose appropriate occupational roles and then play these roles to satisfy their need for achievement. Success through academic achievement may well be very important for them.

Achievement motivation may influence the commitment and enthusiasm which some adults show for formal learning but it is far from being the only motivational factor of importance.

Motivation to Study

Morstain and Smart (1978) investigated the motives which led 626 adult part-time degree students to attend courses. Each student completed an Education Participation Scale which listed 48 possible reasons for participating in educational activities. Subsequent analysis of the responses identified five major reasons for attending college. Just over half the sample appeared to be without any specific goals or purposes; this group were identified as non-directed learners. A quarter of the group were attending for reasons directly connected with their current or future career interests. Nine per cent of the students had scores which suggested they were mainly concerned with creating or improving their social interactions and personal relationships, another nine per cent were attending courses in order to escape the routine and monotony of everyday life and to change their lives in some way, whilst six per cent seemed to be stimulation seekers intent upon escaping from the tedium of daily life by expanding their intellectual horizons.

Obviously the proportion of individuals in each type will have been largely determined by the range and nature of the courses that they had chosen to study; none the less the general motivational typology is of interest as is the finding that each group of adult learners, formed on the basis of their similarity of motivations, exhibited a wide range of demographic characteristics. It was not true, for example, that young men were significantly more career-oriented or older women motivated by the desire to be involved in social service.

The Self-concept and its Influence on Learning

The Origins of the Self-concept

A theme running through much of this chapter has been that the image the individual has of himself affects his approach to, and level of performance in, attempting to deal with many aspects of life. This image which is largely the product of interaction with 'significant others' is often referred to as the self-concept. The self-concept includes three main elements. There is the self-image which is the impression which we have of ourselves, there is the ideal self which is our image of the way we could be or ought to be or would like to be and there is the element of self-esteem which consists of the feelings that we have about the self we believe ourselves to be.

Probably the most significant influence upon the development of the self-image is the acquisition of language between the ages of two and three. The self-image is formed very much like a new concept; it is an abstraction of the common factor from all our personal experiences. The frequent use of our name provides us with a verbal label to which we can attach our dawning awareness of self-identity. Through the use of pronouns such as 'I' and 'me' we also begin to symbolise ourselves and our acts. Cooley (1902) maintains that our self-image is constructed largely from the way we think we see ourselves reflected back from the minds of others. In this looking glass theory of the development of the self-image we gradually come to see ourselves as others treat us. However, not everyone is equally important in helping us form our self-image. Some people are much more significant to us than others; for example, our image of ourself will be far more influenced by the way we think our parents, immediate family and friends see us than by the reflections of strangers. According to Mead (1934) the individual begins by imagining how his behaviour would be viewed by 'significant others' and later creates a synthesis based on his interactions with others over a long period so that eventually he develops his view of an appropriate self-image from the point of view of a 'generalised other'. The view that we develop of ourselves then is not necessarily based upon other people's objective assessment of us but upon our perceptions of what others think of us. If others who are important to us make it clear that they see us as intelligent, helpful and caring, in time we will come to see ourselves in this way and come to behave appropriately. If we are fortunate the self-image that we develop will be one which is positive and which facilitates successful learning. We will feel encouraged to expand, extend, develop, mature and express these capacities which will lead towards a fulfilment of our potentialities, towards Maslow's self-actualisation. On the other hand, if the self-image we are encouraged to adopt is a poor one we may be inhibited from attempting to realise our full potential for the rest of our lives. Maizels (1970) describes the effect that school had upon the self-image of early leavers. 'As many as one in four of these early leavers saw their teachers as indifferent to what they did at school and were glad for them to leave. School had done little to get them to value themselves positively.' Such people will be very reluctant to risk their self-image again in the context of formal education; those who do and eventually attend a course will be sensitive to any hint of a reflection of their lack of worth from their teachers.

As we grow older and have more differentiated roles to play in society these roles will be incorporated into our self-image, for others will respond towards us in ways which are appropriate to our roles. Kuhn (1960) found from the analysis of over a thousand self-descriptions by adults that women most commonly described themselves in terms of family relationships whilst men described themselves in terms of their occupational roles. Redundancy and unemployment will have a very undermining effect upon the self-concept and may reduce the individual's readiness to put his self-image further at risk on training courses.

Unemployment and the Self-concept

Hill (1978) found that the initial response to unemployment was often one of denial and a feeling that nothing much had happened. The individual tends to see himself as having the same occupational identity as he had when he was employed and still describes himself by it. Once it becomes clear that a replacement job will not quickly be found the individual enters an intermediate phase where he modifies his self-image to accept that he is unemployed. The third phase which sets in after nine months to a year, is a settling down to unemployment. The individual adjusts to a domestic and economic routine consistent with long-term unemployment. The loss of confidence which goes with the loss of an occupational identity results in a tendency to withdraw from social contacts. The economic consequences also mean that social activities such as going to the pub or visiting relatives are given up. The family becomes the centre of activity, but the man finds himself playing an increasingly feminine role; taking the children to school, shopping and housework bring his sexual identity under attack. It is not difficult to see that a prolonged period of unemployment may have such a deleterious effect upon an individual's self-image that when he is offered the opportunity to undertake retraining he may have lost all confidence in his ability to cope with the learning and may turn down the opportunity rather than run the risk to his already battered self image that further failure would involve.

Much that was said in the early part of the chapter suggested that the adult would be likely to welcome the chance of new learning and will seek out intellectual challenge even when it leads to no useful outcome. Here we see the other side of the coin, the individual who has been so conditioned by those significant others with whom he has come into contact that he has developed a self-image which inhibits him from taking the risks which are involved in striving towards a full realisation of his potential. Such a person will need the most careful help and encouragement so that some of the damage to his self-image may be repaired and he may move towards realising his potential and become more the person he is capable of becoming.

The Ideal Self: Its Origin and Influence

The self-image is the view of our real self that we carry around with us and which is a corner-stone of our personality. The ideal self is the image we have of the way we hope to be or could be or should be. The image of the ideal self has its origins in the perceptions we have of others' expectations of us. These expectations, which come both from significant individuals in our environment as well as from social institutions such as the school, become internalised into an ideal towards which we feel we ought to strive. They become a conscience which provides us with the possibility of self-guidance. The ideal self also has its origins in our tendency to model ourselves on other people. Young children tend to model themselves upon their parents or other members of the family, perhaps an envied older brother or sister. During adolescence it tends to be glamorous people such as sportsmen, pop-stars or actors who provide the model, but as we enter adulthood the model becomes an imaginary composite individual who has all the qualities we admire.

At various times in our lives we are forced to make decisions which close for us some of the possibilities of what we might have become. Perhaps as children we had an involvement with music which had to be dropped in order to meet the high academic standards that our parents expected of us. Perhaps we suppressed an ambition to become a doctor or an engineer because the length of training seemed too daunting to a fiancee eager to get on with married life. Part of the ideal self is killed off. If the denials of our self that we have made to retain the esteem of others are too great then we may come to feel an inner emptiness, as though something inside us has died. Alternatively we may come to lead a double life, guiltily doing what we want but at the expense of a bad conscience and a constant feeling of restlessness and dissatisfaction. When we have denied too many of our potentialities their expression, our self-image and our ideal self can never match up and we find ourselves permanently in a state of conflict.

Our ideal self is important in determining our level of self-esteem. Self-esteem is concerned with the feelings that we have about our self-image. Where the gap between the self-image and the ideal self is not too great then the individual will be likely to have a reasonably high level of self-esteem. Where the gap is large and the self-image does not measure up at all to the ideal self then self-esteem will be at a low ebb. People low in self-esteem tend to be self-centred, anxious and insecure. They are easily persuaded by others because they have little confidence in themselves; often they are depressed and will set themselves unrealistic goals. The healthiest situation is one where the individual has a moderately small gap between his ideal self and his image of himself. He will then be likely to set himself realistic and realisable goals which once achieved can be revised in an upward direction. Basically self-esteem has its origins in successfully achieving the goals which we set ourselves as a result of our conception of our ideal self. The working-class woman who passes her first 'O' level exam at 55 may feel a greater fillip to her self esteem than the 21-year-old who gets an Upper Second when she was expecting a First in her degree exams. Many adults return to formal education in an effort to bring their self-image closer to their view of their ideal self and hence to improve their self-esteem.

Ageing and Learning

The factors that we have considered so far in this chapter are likely to have an influence on our willingness to undertake learning at any stage of our adult life. After the age of about 40, as we begin to enter the second half of our active working life, the effects of the process of ageing begin to have an influence on the facility with which we learn. We have already met the idea of fluid and crystallised intelligence in Chapter 7. Fluid abilities are those which reflect the individual's inborn potentialities whilst the crystallised abilities are those which reflect the way in which education and experience have shaped the fluid abilities. It is the area of fluid intelligence which is most influenced by ageing. Tasks which are unfamiliar, involve working to strict time limits, require the understanding of abstract principles or complex relationships or require the interpretation of symbolic material or its translation from one medium to another are all subject to the adverse effects of ageing. The deterioration is not normally sudden unless the individual suffers an injury or from serious disease, but by the age of 50, on average, the effects of ageing will be noticeable if the individual is pushed to the limits of his mental capacity.

Our ability to perform skills such as driving a car, playing tennis or operating complex equipment also suffers as we advance through middle age. There is a worsening in sensory discrimination that follows from the deterioration in our vision and hearing, there is also a decrement in our physical capabilities. Our muscular strength, speed, stamina and co-ordination all suffer from the effects of the ageing process. Surprisingly these are not the major cause of our worsening skills performance. The major impairment is to the organising and decision-making processes at the level of the central nervous system. The older person is slower in his actions because of a slowing in the central processes involved in perceiving signals and in selecting actions in response to items. These changes set limits to the speed of performance much lower than those set by any muscular changes (Welford, 1958, 1962; Bromley, 1974).

In reality of course people have their day to day lives organised in such a way that they can deal with most contingencies by drawing upon familiar and well-practised routines, which can be carried out at their own pace.

Older people also often develop strategies that compensate for their deteriorating abilities. For example, they may avoid driving in demanding traffic conditions, or give up playing competitive tennis if they feel such tasks are placing demands upon them that exceed their capabilities. As a result the adverse effects of their decline do not become obvious until later in life. However, if an older person finds himself in a formal learning situation, such as a retraining programme, then he may well experience the impact of these changes upon his ability to learn especially if the designers of the programme have done nothing to compensate for the difficulties of the older learner. With a well designed training programme there is no reason why the older learner should not work within his limits and probably reach a standard of performance comparable to that of the younger learner. The younger person will reach a level of performance which still leaves him with spare capacity while the older person may be operating closer to his limits (Newsham, 1969; Belbin, 1964).

There is considerable variation between individuals in their approach, performance and commitment to learning. In this chapter and the preceding one we have considered a number of factors which may account for some of these differences. Often the differences have their origins in the basic personality structures of the individual and many of the factors we have considered interrelate although it is far beyond the scope of this book to consider such interactions in detail. If there is one theme that clearly emerges it is that there can be no easy straightforward generalisations about the needs and characteristics of the adult learner. Each individual is unique and his learning will be most effective when his personal strengths and weaknesses are acknowledged and taken into account.

9 THE SOCIAL CONTEXT OF ADULT LEARNING

The Social Climate and Individual Learning

A great deal of adult learning is of the incidental kind; it happens as a consequence of the individual engaging in his day to day activities without any deliberate or conscious decision on his part to learn something new. Such, for instance, is the learning of the housewife or motorist who comes to recognise what volume of liquid makes a litre because only litre or half litre packs of orange juice or oil are on sale, or the learning of the social security claimant who discovers the routines to follow to obtain unemployment benefit when he finds himself out of a job. The psychological processes that are at work in the individual when this unstructured, incidental learning comes about are not basically any different to the processes that go on when the learning is more formal and undertaken deliberately in an educational or training setting. The major difference is that the informal learning is usually very much under the control of the learner. Sometimes when the learning is solely the result of trial and error it is far from efficient. Left to our own devices we may by trial and error work out a way to plaster a wall, but it is very improbable that without instruction we will ever learn to do it with the speed and efficiency of the formally trained plasterer. On other occasions, if our interest and motivation is high enough, we may seek out innumerable sources of information for ourselves and become experts. The enthusiast for war games may come to know more about the military history of a period than any available academic course would be likely to teach him. In informal learning the individual often determines his own approach to his learning.

With formal learning there is far more likely to be a teacher or instructor and a whole social context mediating the way in which the individual approaches his learning. In formal education or training settings the social climate of the institution or organisation may have a considerable influence upon the individual's learning as may also the way the teacher relates to his students and the immediate social context within which the learning takes place, such as the lecture or discussion group. In this chapter we will turn our attention to some of the possible influences of the social context for formal instruction upon the quality and effectiveness of adult learning.

121

Educational and training institutions show marked differences in social climate. Even parallel institutions ostensibly working towards the same educational goals may vary markedly, one seeming a friendly and welcoming place where students and teachers are on easy terms with each other whilst another may have a formal and rather hostile atmosphere where the teachers keep themselves apart and the students seem subdued and rather resentful. It is clear that where such differences in climate exist they will have a marked effect on the students' attitudes towards the institution, towards academic achievement and towards their willingness to work toward the achievement of the institution's objectives.

Each educational setting, whether it is a university, polytechnic, adult education institute or company training workshop has its own climate which derives from the whole spectrum of more or less separate sub-cultures which in various ways affect the behaviour and performance of the learners. The climate of an organisation consists of a combination of all the organisational factors and of all the personality characteristics of the members of the organisation. Thus although it is comparatively easy to recognise the differences in the climates of organisations especially if they are performing similar functions, it is far from easy to unravel the causes of such differences or to demonstrate how different characteristics of the organisation and its members influence the climate.

Factors Influencing Social Climate

Backman and Secord (1968) have suggested that there are three major factors that determine the climate of an educational institution. First, there are the characteristics of the students joining the institution. These include personality variables, abilities, motives, values, career and educational aspirations and their past experiences especially in other institutions. Secondly, there are the characteristics of the institution itself. These include the size, the way authority is exercised, the facilities available, the nature of the setting of the institution, for example, whether it is all on one site or residential, as well as the norms, values and role requirements of the institution — is it meant to give a general education or produce qualified gas-fitters or even do both? Thirdly, there are the characteristics of the informal organisation that exists within the institution. This includes the values and norms that are expressed through the traditions and collective feelings that are passed from one generation of students to another.

Probably the most disparate of these three factors, especially with a heterogeneous organisation such as a large university or polytechnic will be the characteristics of the incoming students. In contrast a training workshop within a factory will probably have a much smaller difference in student background, for most people will come with very much the same educational and social background.

The three factors are not independent of each other but interact to a greater or lesser extent dependent upon circumstances. In the case of some formal educational institutions there is some degree of self-selection amongst students. For example, one individual will see a particular polytechnic with its emphasis on practical work experience as an integral part of its engineering courses as being the ideal place for him, whilst another more theoretically-oriented student will attempt to enrol in another institution which has a reputation for being theoretically-oriented in its teaching of engineering. Thus the characteristics of the entering students may, at least to some extent, be influenced by the characteristics of the institution. Once they have joined the students may react differently to the formal and informal characteristics of the institution. The formally stated norms of the institution, for example, may include the undertaking of a considerable amount of independent study in the student's non-time-tabled time, but the informal norm amongst a large sub-group of students may be to spend most of this time actively engaged in a variety of extra-curricular activities. In a study of the way college of education students spent their time it was found that students gaining high academic grades spent significantly more time in private study than students gaining lower academic grades (Ward, 1973). It is likely that those students who spent more time in private study were responding to the formal characteristics of the institution whilst those who spent the minimum time in private study were probably responding more to the informal traditions of a student sub-group. The individual characteristics of the student may make him more receptive to some aspects of the climate of an institution and more resistant to others. This receptivity will determine to what extent he responds to the formal characteristics of the institution and to what extent he responds to the traditions and norms of student sub-groups. To some extent his need for affiliation and his desire to be accepted by particular sub-groups will be relevant to his behaviour here. Groups can satisfy very important needs for us and because they are so important they can put us under great pressure to conform. Freedman (1967) in a review of the literature on climates that encourage learning says that students are more influenced by their fellow students than by any other factor in the educational institution.

The academic goals and processes of colleges are in large measure transmitted to new students by the predominant student culture. The climate of an educational institution can have a marked influence on how the individual approaches his learning but because of individual differences it will certainly not influence all individuals uniformly.

Schmuck (1966) in a study involving a wide age range of school children has shown that the teachers with positive social climates in their class-rooms regarded their students as individuals rather than merely as members of a group. They emphasised their students' psychological attributes. These teachers talked with a wide variety of their students more often than was the case with other teachers and they rewarded their students individually. When they meted out punishments it was to the class as a whole. In contrast the teachers who had negative social climates rarely talked to students and then to only a few. These teachers very rarely issued rewards and punished individual students in public.

Older People, Social Climate and Learning

Many older people coming to formal study for the first time after an interval of many years will be particularly sensitive to the climate of the institution. For many people schooldays were not an especially happy time; the competitive atmosphere of class grades and examinations to be passed has left them with the feeling that they were less than completely successful at school. For many, especially the less educationally successful, the processes of classical conditioning that we met in Chapter 2 will have left them with strong emotional feelings about undertaking formal learning. If, on joining the educational institution, they are reminded of the atmosphere that they disliked about school then all the old antipathies and anxieties will be aroused. If, however, they feel the climate is noticeably different, that the teachers are approachable equals welcoming them rather than authoritarian figures likely to sit in judgement over them, then they will be more relaxed and prepared to take the risks to their self-esteem that undertaking formal learning so often involves for the mature adult.

A study by Newsham (1969) which compared the labour turnover of middle-aged trainees with that of younger people suggested that amongst older workers the methods adopted for training had a greater significance as an influence upon their continued employment than was the case with younger people. Older trainees in industry typically lacked confidence in their abilities to cope with their training. In such a situation it is crucial that everything possible is done to create a friendly and supportive atmosphere in the training institution. Older trainees appreciate having written instructions available so that they can refer to them whenever they begin to have doubts about their recollection of what to do. Introducing production material too soon on the course can heighten feelings of anxiety. It is better to provide the older learner with a longer induction period and to allow him to come to terms gradually with both new equipment and machinery and with new jobs. In this way he will never come to feel overwhelmed or feel that things are beyond his ability to cope with. It helps if groups of workmates can be recruited together; in this way the individual can gain support from friends who are in the same challenging situation as himself. He will lose less face if he is with familiar, sympathetic people should he not succeed first time.

It is also important to avoid formal tests and blackboard and classroom situations which will remind the trainee of situations in which he has experienced a sense of failure in the past. The way in which subject matter is presented should relate to the experience of the trainee. New knowledge is often best presented as a solution to a problem which is already appreciated by the trainee. In this way it is integrated readily with the ideas which are already in the long-term memory store. Older trainees do not like to have the pressures that come from being paced or working to a tight time-table. They much prefer to be allowed to work at their own pace attempting to improve upon their own previous performances rather than working to formal time limits with targets that have been set by others. The climate in the training institution can make all the difference to whether the older person is successfully retrained or whether he seeks out instead a job that makes no demands in the way of formal learning but which almost invariably means a lowering of his economic status.

Leadership and Social Climate

The teachers in an institution contribute significantly towards the creation of the social climate by the way they carry out their leadership roles with the various groups that they encounter. Of course leadership in educational settings is not attached exclusively to the formally appointed teachers; there are occasions when the students themselves may quite properly exercise leadership roles. We will now turn our attention to the influence of leadership styles upon the way individuals behave in groups and hence upon the experiences they will be likely to have.

The leader of a group is the member who has the most influence over the behaviour of other members. Some leaders such as teachers are appointed; they hold their office formally and derive at least some of their authority from their position. Other leaders are emergent; they come forward as leaders from within the group in an informal way as a result of the interactions between the group members. Many groups have a formally appointed leader and an emergent or informal leader and in such a case it is usually the emergent leader who is the real centre of power within the group. He is the person the group have chosen as leader rather than had imposed upon them.

Leaders have many functions that they carry out for the group. Krech, Crutchfield and Ballachey (1962) identified the following as amongst the functions a group may want its leader to fulfil: 'executive, planner, policy maker, expert, external group representative, controller of internal relations, purveyor of rewards and punishments, arbitrator and mediator, exemplar, symbol of the group, substitute for individual responsibility, ideologist, father-figure and scapegoat'. In most group situations it is not possible for one person to carry out all these functions and they tend to be shared around amongst the group members. The more important leadership functions however tend to become centred around two particular roles which Bales and Slater (1955) identified as those of the task specialist and the socio-emotional specialist. The task leader is the person who specialises in recognising and diagnosing problems that stand between the group and its objectives. He initiates and plans, he directs the group towards achieving its objectives and in doing so often forces members to change their behaviour and to re-examine their ideas and values. As a result of this he often creates tension within the group and by forcing members to behave in ways that they would not otherwise choose he sometimes exacerbates tensions between group members. It is now that the socio-emotional leader comes into his own. It is his role to maintain unity and morale within the group, to improve the communications between group members and to reduce tensions and friction within the group. The task leader helps the group achieve the objectives or goals for which it originally came into existence whilst the socio-emotional leader looks after the internal well-being of the group.

In some situations it is possible for the leader to play roles of both task and socio-emotional leadership but more often than not these two roles are carried out by different individuals. In many groups where formal adult learning is the prime objective for the group's existence it is the formally appointed teacher who is the task leader whilst the socio-emotional leadership role will be largely taken over by one or perhaps more emergent leaders who come from the student group.

Effects of Leadership Style

Different individuals adopt different leadership styles. We will now consider some of the evidence which relates the effectiveness of the group to the way the leader behaves. Lewin, Lippitt and White (1939) set up four groups of ten-year-old boys with five boys in each group and got them to meet regularly after school for activities such as mural painting, soap carving and model airplane construction. Four adult leaders were rotated from group to group at six-weekly intervals and on each change adopted a different leadership style so each group experienced each leadership style from different leaders. Three leadership styles were adopted: democratic, authoritarian and *laissez-faire*. The democratic leader ensured that all policies were a matter of group discussion; he sketched the general steps needed to reach the group goal but left the detailed procedures to the choice of the group; he allowed freedom to choose work partners and was as objective as possible in his praise and criticism. He tried to be a group member in spirit without doing too much of the work. In his authoritarian role the leader imposed policy on the group; he prescribed the techniques and organisation of activities and dictated the work companions of each member. He was personal in his praise and criticism and remained aloof from the group unless demonstrating. When playing a *laissez-faire* leadership role he supplied materials but gave complete freedom for group or individual decisions, made infrequent comments and was completely non-participatory. When faced with a *laissez-faire* leader groups did less work and its quality was poor. With an authoritarian leader the groups were at their most productive, but they were either submissive towards or dependent upon the leader and unfriendly towards each other. When the leader left the room the groups stopped working on the task in hand. Under democratic leadership the groups were more contented and continued to work when the leader was not present.

Throughout the forties and fifties the basic procedures of the above experiments were repeated with numerous groups and much the same findings were obtained: that democratic leadership although less productive resulted in higher morale and was preferred by the group members. Interesting as these findings are they should not be accepted uncritically. Anderson (1959) reviewed 49 of these studies and came to the conclusion the 'the authoritarian-democratic construct is an inadequate basis for research because, for one thing, it presumes to summarise the complexity of group life into a single dimension.' Lewin, Lippitt and White's work was too simple but none the less it was on useful lines.

Fiedler (1962, 1965) attempted to explore more comprehensively the complexity of the relationship between leadership and group performance. Fiedler set out to relate leadership style to group productivity. Group leaders were scored on a bipolar scale. A high scorer tended to be accepting, permissive, considerate, anxiety reducing and person-oriented: note here the similarities with the democratic leader. A low scoring leader tended to be directive, controlling, managing, anxiety-inducing and task-oriented in his dealings with his group: in other words much like the authoritarian leader. Fiedler reviewed the productivity of a large number of different task groups in the light of the different leadership styles which were adopted. He found that the results were complicated by three other factors. First, there were differences in the relations between the leader and the members. In some groups the leader experienced the group as pleasant and friendly towards him while in others the group had poor relations with their leader. Secondly, there was a variation in the degree to which the task could be structured. In a highly structured situation there were clear goals, with verifiable results and clear-cut procedures to be followed, for example, firing an anti-aircraft gun or launching a boat. In other situations the task was unstructured with many possible ways of proceeding, as for example in writing a review sketch. Thirdly, the power of the leader's position varied from one group to another. In some contexts the leader's authority was backed up by rules and he had control over the dispensation of rewards and punishment. For example, an army officer is in a strong position whilst the elected leader in a youth club is in a weak position.

Taking these three factors of leader-member relations, task structure and power of the leader into account, Fiedler found that the directing, task-oriented, autocratic leader had the highest productivity both when most factors were in his favour (for example, when the leader-member relations were good, the task was structured and his position was strong) and when most factors were against him (for example, when his relations within the group were poor, the task was unstructured and his position was weak). When however the mixture of these factors added up to only a moderately favourable situation for the leader then the permissive, considerate, person-oriented, 'democratic' leader obtained the greatest productivity from his group.

Fiedler's model emphasises that different situations require different leadership styles. A teacher who has good relations with his group but has no great power over them would do best to use a 'democratic' person-oriented approach if he were dealing with a comparatively unstructured task such as leading a group discussion about a novel his students had read. If, however, the other factors remained unchanged and he was working on a highly structured task, say teaching his students a new swimming stroke, then he would do better to adopt a more controlling, task-oriented 'authoritarian' approach. If he is to help people to get the best out of the learning experiences that group work can offer, the group leader needs to have a flexibility of leadership style so that he can change from a task-oriented to a person-oriented emphasis as the learning context demands.

Social Settings and Learning

There is a large range of different teaching approaches that are used in formal educational settings, some involving the teacher in taking most of the initiative whilst the students remain fairly passive, as in formal lectures, others involving far more active student participation, as in discussion groups. In the final section of this chapter we will review some of the more frequently used ways of organising the social contexts within which formal teaching takes place and consider the possible influences of these different approaches upon the quality and effectiveness of the student learning.

All forms of teaching involve some interaction between the teacher and learner. In most formal learning settings there are a number of learners involved with the teacher at any one time and in some settings there is some degree of interaction between the students.

The Lecture

The lecture is the method of teaching which most readily comes to mind when people think about formal learning. A lecture can be a very economical way of teaching; indeed with the use of closed circuit television and video tape-recording many hundreds of people may learn from the same lecture. Bligh (1972) in a very comprehensive study of the lecture found it to be an effective way to teach factual information. A lecture can be used to give a general framework for the study of a subject.

An able lecturer may be able to use the technique to achieve other aims as well. One lecturer may demonstrate the techniques that he might use in handling evidence, taking the students through his thought processes step by step as he considers and evaluates alternative hypotheses. Another may have evolved a more inspirational style, using his talents as an actor to generate an enthusiasm for his subject which is then carried over into other modes of study. Successful lecturing is more dependent upon the skill of the lecturer than upon the ideas that are being presented. It is not at all an effective way to teach students to think for themselves. In the formal lecture the teacher speaks and the students listen passively, possibly taking notes on what the lecturer is saying. The communication is almost exclusively one way, from the lecturer to the students. The lecturer must present the same content to all the students no matter what their previous experience or familiarity with the subject matter; it is structured in the way that he chooses at a pace that is under his control. In some situations it is possible for the lecturer to obtain some guidance as to how his audience is responding, from non-verbal cues such as facial expressions, degree of attentiveness and rate of note taking. Questions if they come are from individuals; the rest of the audience eavesdrop on the reply, but there is no possibility for the lecturer to take any fuller account of the special needs of individuals. He has no sure indication at the time his lecture is being delivered whether the audience have understood what he has been saying to them or not. The student learning is passive and the lecturer's word often seems to have a finality to the student which the lecturer would probably not wish it to have. Because the ideas presented are structured to suit the lecturer they are not necessarily easily integrated into the student's conceptual structures in long-term memory. With the lecture, learning is at second hand. No lecturer would be happy to think that his students learned exclusively from lecture notes yet a study by Schonell, Roe and Middleton (1962) found that 15 per cent of students in some higher education institutions in Australia were relying exclusively upon their lecture notes whilst the majority supplemented their notes with only the minimum of further study.

The Lesson

One common variant of the formal lecture which overcomes some of its limitations is that of the class-room lesson. The teacher is still the main source of information and the communication is still largely one way — from the teacher to the student — but here the students are encouraged to ask questions if they do not understand the ideas that are being presented. From time to time the teacher will also ask questions of individuals to test their comprehension and will adapt his lesson material if necessary to cope with the misunderstandings that he has detected. However, there is no guarantee that the feedback the teacher gets from individuals is typical of the majority of the class. For example, one very able student who already has a strong grasp of the subject matter being presented may engage the teacher with numerous questions. The teacher may modify his presentation to meet the needs of this student whilst other class members are left in a state of increasing confusion which they may be too modest to confess.

A number of very successful methods have been developed for improving the quantity and quality of the feedback that is available to the class teacher. Some involve presenting all the students with questions which they must answer in written form during the lesson and they are then given details of the correct answers immediately. One adaptable and economical way of obtaining feedback about student understanding uses a device known as the Cosford cube. Students are provided with a two and a half inch cube with differently coloured faces. The student answers multiple choice questions about the lesson material by turning an appropriately coloured cube-face towards the teacher. In this way the teacher can obtain immediate feedback about the understanding of all his students. All these methods of augmenting feedback for the teacher appear to improve the quality of learning (Beard, Bligh and Harding, 1978).

Group Discussion and Seminar

With the group discussion or seminar the teacher is no longer the chief source of information and ideas. In an effective discussion the teacher engineers a social situation in which all the students are prepared to contribute. Anyone taking part in the discussion may supply information, anyone can ask questions either of the group as a whole or of individual members of the group. Any member of the group should be free to attempt to answer questions or to clarify others' misunderstandings. The members learn from each other. If the climate of the group is a friendly and supportive one, then individuals will be prepared to risk revealing their ignorance or misconceptions without fear of losing self-esteem.

For a discussion to be successful it is necessary for the teacher to have clear aims about what he wishes the discussion to achieve. Students for their part must come to a discussion with something useful to contribute. If discussion is to be used as a way of teaching an academic discipline, then the students must have done some preparatory work before they come to the discussion group. No group can sit down and discuss the economic consequences of the Franco-Prussian war in a useful way unless the participants have attempted to establish for themselves in advance what the consequences were. The preparatory work done by each individual need not cover exactly the same ground. The discussion provides an opportunity for an enrichment and deepening of each individual's understanding from the opportunity to hear others' interpretations of the evidence they have uncovered. A good discussion will give the participants an opportunity to hear and actively explore in terms of their own cognitive structures a range of points of view. In a successful discussion the students' learning is active, but if the participants' preparation is inadequate for them to contribute satisfactorily or if the leader of the group fails to keep the aims of the discussion clearly in mind then very little may be gained from this method.

Tutorials

Individual tutorial work is often used in higher education. With this teaching method a small number of students, or perhaps only one, come to discuss some particular aspect of their work with the teacher. This method results in considerable work by the student, at least during the tutorial. The interplay of minds concentrating on a particular area means that a subject can often be pursued in considerable depth. It can also provide an excellent opportunity for the student to seek individual expert help with any difficulties in his understanding of the subject matter being studied. However, this is a very uneconomical method in terms of demands on staff time and some students feel intimidated by the concentrated attention of the teacher. If the individual student and teacher do not get on well together, then the difficulties of the social relationship may interfere considerably with the student's learning.

Role-play, Simulation and Games

The basic approach of all three of these techniques is the same: the students are given an opportunity to learn by experiencing at least to some degree some aspects of another person's world. With a role-play one or more students are given a briefing about a social situation. They are asked to imagine themselves in the roles of the participants and they then improvise and act out the encounter. For example, two social workers in training may be asked to role-play an interview between a social worker and a client. After the role-play the participants will be given an opportunity to analyse the way that they behaved when they were in their roles. The chance role-play provides to get inside someone else's skin for a brief time may help the learner to gain insight into the motivation and feelings of another person that no lecture or discussion could ever provide.

In a simulation the teacher presents his group with many of the elements of a real-life problem in as realistic a way as possible. For example, a simulation exercise as part of a management course may face the group with an industrial relations problem. The students will be given as much relevant information about the problem as possible and then either through role-play or through individual work or group discussion, they will be asked to attempt to find a solution to the problem. Some simulation exercises may take a considerable time to work through with new information or facets to the problem being added as the students progress. Games are simulations with a competitive element. There are rules, points are awarded and there are winners and losers. Both games and simulations enable the students to learn by experiencing at first hand at least some of the elements of realistic problems. They are ideal for showing how systems work and drawing attention to cause and effect. As with role-play, simulation and games need to be followed by a period when the students can discuss, evaluate and rethink in detail the way that they approached the exercise. If this debriefing does not happen and the students do not attempt to integrate their experiences with their previous knowledge and understanding then these exercises are a waste of time. The closer to reality that a role-play, simulation or game comes the more successful it is likely to be (Taylor and Walford 1972; Longley 1972).

Laboratory and Practical Work

Laboratory work in the sciences or practical work in subjects as varied as catering, engineering and medicine all enable the students to learn through personal experience and concrete activities. Such methods are often time-consuming, for the students do not necessarily learn just because they are doing. For effective learning in practical situations the students need to have a clear idea of what their activities are meant to achieve. They will also need help with evaluating the success of their actions in the early stages of mastering practical skills, as we saw in Chapter 6.

Projects

Project work normally involves students in investigating some area of study in detail. Projects can be used in almost any area of training. The best projects enable students to exploit their existing knowledge and experience by using it to break new ground. An architect working on a project to design a new modular house or an engineer working on a project to produce a man-powered flying machine will draw upon a whole range of subjects and sources of information and will be forced to integrate them in a new and original way. The personal involvement and commitment that students often feel towards their project may considerably increase their motivation. However projects can be very time consuming and unless they are carefully directed they can impose a great strain on a student without much of real worth being achieved.

In the latter part of this chapter we have looked briefly at a number of the more common methods which the teacher may use to help his students towards a mastery of the subject matter that they are studying. There are also other ways of presenting subject matter which we have not discussed. There is no ideal method for teaching; each technique we have considered has its advantages and its disadvantages. Some techniques are more suitable to one kind of subject rather than another. The best teaching will come about when the teacher chooses from amongst the techniques he has at his disposal those that best meet the special characteristics of both the subject matter and the learner. In the next and final chapter we will explore the importance for the teacher of adults of considering objectives, content, teaching methods and student characteristics as an integrated whole.

10 PLANNING AND EVALUATING ADULT LEARNING

Planning Teaching

As we have seen earlier in this book there are many factors which influence the way an adult will approach a learning task. Some are the consequences of previous learning and experience, some result from personal disposition and yet others may be due to the social context within which the learning is to take place. The successful teacher of adults will attempt to take as many of these factors as possible into account in his teaching. Although individual differences between one learner and another may be complex they represent only some of the variables that the teacher needs to reckon with when planning his teaching. In this final chapter we will explore some of the decisions the teacher must make if his instruction is to be successful.

There are three major and closely interrelated areas in which the teacher must make decisions: his first concern must be to identify in as much detail as he finds helpful what it is that is to be learned and how he will evaluate whether successful learning has taken place. Once these overall aims and major objectives are established he will have to make decisions about the order and sequence in which the subject matter is to be presented. Finally, he will need to make decisions about the teaching methods and student activities that will best help him meet his aims and objectives.

Before these decisions can be made there are many judgements that the teacher must attempt to make about the characteristics of his students and the nature of the subject matter to be taught. He must consider the existing knowledge and conceptual structure of the students in the area of the learning. He must take into account both the best logical order and the best psychological order when thinking about the sequencing of subject matter. Also he must make judgements, bearing in mind the factors we have explored in earlier chapters, about which teaching approaches would be most likely to suit the students he is to work with. We will now explore the three areas of aims and objectives, sequencing subject matter and selecting teaching methods in more detail.

Aims and Objectives

Before a teacher can plan the detail of his teaching he must first decide

135

upon the goals that he intends his students to reach by the end of the course. These long-term goals represent his aims for the course. In many cases he will have a syllabus or a course programme to give him general guidelines but within these guidelines there is often considerable freedom for personal interpretation. Once the overall aims are determined the teacher can begin to consider his detailed objectives for each lesson or teaching session. Until the teacher has clearly established what the students are to learn he can go no further in his planning and decision-making.

There is considerable difference of opinion amongst teachers about how explicitly aims and objectives should be or can be stated. Mager (1970) has argued that objectives should be written by identifying as precisely as possible the new behaviour that the learner should be able to produce after the learning experience. Without clearly defined behavioural objectives, he claims, it is impossible to evaluate a course efficiently and there is no firm basis for the selection of teaching materials, detailed content or teaching methods. When objectives are defined with precision the student can use them to evaluate his own progress and hence will be more likely to engage in activities that will contribute to his success in achieving the objectives. In one study with newly graduated engineers who were attending an in-company training course before being permanently assigned to their positions, Mager and McCann (1963) reduced training time by 65 per cent on a course that normally lasted six months, as a result of giving the students the detailed course objectives. The students were able to fill in the gap between what they already knew and what they needed to know without wasting time relearning what was already familiar.

One of the most influential books in the area of curriculum development in recent years has been Bloom's *Taxonomy of Educational Objectives: the Classification of Educational Goals*. The *Taxonomy* was published in two parts, the first covering educational objectives in the cognitive domain (Bloom, 1956) and the second covering objectives in the affective domain (Krathwohl *et al.*, 1964). This book offered teachers a classificatory system which was intended to help them to identify educational goals in the form of observable student behaviour. Bloom's approach has been used, often in modified form, by many teachers (Beard, 1967). In many courses, especially in technical colleges, there is now great emphasis upon stating instructional objectives in such a way that it is possible to decide whether they have been achieved from the behaviour of the students after the lesson or course. Behavioural objectives are expressed in terms of what the learner will be able to do as a result of his learning. Descriptions such as to write, to recite, to identify, to construct or to list are acceptable whilst descriptions such as to know, to understand, to appreciate, to enjoy or to believe are considered open to too many interpretations to be helpful.

The precision with which instructional objectives can be stated in behavioural terms varies for different subjects and activities. It is easy to be precise about the behavioural changes you expect in students who are learning factual information: after the period of learning they should be able to list or state the facts that they have learned. It is less easy to identify the behavioural objectives that are to be achieved from more open-ended activities that are intended to promote creative thought or artistic endeavour. The art teacher may recognise original and creative work when a student produces it but will be likely to find it difficult, if not impossible, to state precise behavioural objectives that will enable him to discriminate between outstanding work and the competent but more mediocre work of the majority of the students. With such activities it is often possible to do no more than to state the outline of the main course objectives. Whatever the difficulties of stating objectives in behavioural terms it is obviously important that teachers should be as precise as possible in defining the learning they hope to bring about with each topic or lesson.

The Roles of Evaluation

Once the aims and objectives for the course are established the teacher must attempt to make an evaluation of what the students will bring to the learning. In some cases the teacher will have detailed knowledge of the students' relevant previous achievements in the area of study. Such would be the case if the teacher had taught the students on an earlier related course, or if the new students were highly similar in educational experience to others he has taught in the past. In other circumstances the teacher can only identify the students' existing state of knowledge after he has talked with them at length or made a formal assessment. This initial evaluation will also include attempting to identify where the individual students stand in relation to factors such as personality, attitudes, degree of motivation and cognitive style. In some circumstances the teacher may need to revise his objectives once he has made these initial evaluations. For example, if he finds that his students have insufficient background knowledge to cover the ground as quickly as he had intended, he will need to select less ambitious objectives.

When his initial evaluations are as complete as possible the teacher should be in a position to decide what and how much material can be presented in each learning sequence and to decide what teaching methods and learning activities on the part of his students are most likely to lead to the achievement of the objectives. The teacher should now be in a position to plan the detail of his early teaching sequences.

Once his teaching begins the teacher needs to make frequent evaluations of his students' progress with their learning. These evaluations will sometimes be made formally through tests but often they are the result of informal observations of the students' progress and responses to questions. As a result of evaluation made during the teaching sequence the teacher will make an assessment as best he can of current progress and will also make a diagnosis of what still remains to be learned. At this stage the teacher may need to revise his objectives if he finds his students are not making the progress with their learning that he had originally anticipated. He will also exploit what he has learned from this ongoing assessment in planning the detail of his subsequent teaching.

As he comes to the end of his work with his students, the teacher will attempt to evaluate the extent to which his overall objectives have been achieved both by the individual learners and by the group as a whole. The detailed description of the methods used in the evaluation of learning is complex (Gronlund, 1976; Thyne, 1974) and is beyond the scope of this book. Evaluation involves much more than a mere collection of techniques; it should be a continuous process underlying all good teaching and learning. The key to effective evaluation is to be found in clearly stated objectives for student learning. We cannot tell what progress we have made towards our destination until we are clear about where we are going.

Sequencing Subject Matter

The teacher must decide both the order in which to present the different topics that are to be taught on his course and also the order in which to present the detailed information within each topic. We will now consider some of the general principles that are relevant to the sequencing of subject matter.

As we saw in Chapter 3, material which can be fitted into the existing conceptual structures in the long-term memory of the individual has a much better chance of being retained accurately over long periods of time than does the isolated fact that cannot easily be linked to existing knowledge. The teacher must attempt to select, organise and present new learning in such a way that the learner can readily appreciate its relationship to ideas he already has in his long-term memory. In this way the new ideas, information and skills will stand the best chance of becoming part of an integrated and organised body of knowledge in the mind of the learner. Few adults ever come to a new learning task with no useful knowledge available. Mager and Clark (1963) found that when they tested the skill of a group of housewives at electrical meter reading their average score was 40 per cent. All the subjects claimed ignorance of this area of electronics and of meter reading. In spite of this their performances were half as good as those of experts. These housewives would have entered a training course with a considerable amount of existing relevant knowledge even though it was probably obtained as the result of incidental learning.

Even if the teacher can assess accurately the student's existing relevant knowledge before he begins his new learning, he will still find it very difficult to view the new material from the point of view of the learner. A person who is thoroughly familiar with a subject will often find it very hard to anticipate those aspects of the subject likely to cause the newcomer problems. The following experiment illustrates this point. Mager (1961) arranged for one student at a time to be given complete control over a curriculum in electronics. The instructor responded to student questions but gave no unsolicited information, instruction or explanation. The learner selected for himself the subjects he wanted to discuss, the depth to which he wished to take them, the kinds of equipment and demonstrations he felt would be useful and the frequency and nature of reviews of his progress. Mager found that subjects selected a sequence of information that was considerably different from that of the traditional electronics curriculum. The teacher should not assume that the order he, the expert, would select for the presentation of subject matter is necessarily the one that will best suit the existing cognitive structures of his students.

With some subject matter there appears to be a logical order for the presentation of ideas. In chemistry we would expect to study the properties of the basic elements before going on to study compound materials and in biology the study of simpler organisms seems to come logically before the study of more complex animals such as mammals. However, this logical ordering may not be the most suitable psychologically. As we noted earlier, the successful long-term retention of new learning is dependent upon the cognitive structures that are available within the learner's long-term memory. If the learner already has a rich network of interrelated concepts in connection with compound materials or with mammals, then the teacher may find that the student learning is more efficient if this existing knowledge can be used as the starting point.

One of the oldest rules of teaching is that the teacher should take the student from where he is to where the teacher wants him to be. Instruction should start at the edge of the student's knowledge. To ignore what the student knows already or to start beyond the edge of his knowledge is to create unnecessary obstacles for him. To begin within the student's knowledge is to bore him. Sticking firmly to the logical or traditional sequence for the presentation of subject matter and ignoring the psychological dimension that results from previous learning may well cause avoidable problems.

The Relationship Between New and Existing Knowledge

Ausubel *et al.* (1978) have stressed that if new learning is to be meaningful it must be related to what is already known by the student. Information that cannot be related to conceptual structures already in the long-term memory must be rote learned. Rote learning is less efficient than meaningful learning; it takes longer and information that is rote learned is less likely to be retained for long periods because it gets no support from other information in memory.

Before he plans the detail of the teaching of his subject matter the teacher should determine which concepts his students must know for the new material to be meaningful to them. If they do not have these concepts available, he will need to introduce them before he moves on to the main content of his teaching. The sequencing of subject matter should be planned in such a way that new concepts can be related to ones which have preceded them. If important concepts are omitted by the teacher or are not successfully learned by the student, new ideas which are dependent upon them for meaning will require more effort to get into long-term memory and will be more vulnerable to forgetting.

There are occasions when the student does have relevant existing knowledge in his long-term memory but fails to recognise its relationship with his new learning. It is not sufficient merely to have relevant concepts in the memory, they need to be readily available for recall if they are to be of help in establishing the new learning.

Advance Organisers

Ausubel *et al.* (1978) have advocated the use of organisers introduced in advance of the new learning material which establish a meaningful learning set in the mind of the student. So that they can function effectively for a range of students, each of whom will have an idiosyncratic organisation to his cognitive structure dependent upon his past learning experiences these advance organisers, according to Ausubel, should be at a higher level of abstraction, generality and inclusiveness than the new material which is to be learned. The principal function of the advance organiser is to provide a scaffolding of ideas to bridge the gap between what the student already knows and what he needs to know before he can learn the new material in a meaningful fashion. This scaffolding of higher level ideas allows the incorporation into a stable structure of the more detailed and differentiated material that follows in the learning session.

Ausubel sees three different functions for advance organisers. First, they draw upon and mobilise whatever relevant concepts the student may have in his conceptual structure; secondly, they make it possible to fit the new learning into a higher order conceptual structure which helps retention and thirdly, they make rote learning unnecessary because they provide the student with key ideas on which to anchor his new learning.

Advance organisers seem to be most effective when students have little prior knowledge which can be used to organise or subsume the new material that is to be learned (Grotelueschen and Sjorgren, 1968; Kuhn and Novak, 1971). If the student already has a useful conceptual structure that can be used to anchor the new material then the advance organiser serves little purpose.

Progressive Differentiation and Integrative Reconciliation

There are two further principles which Ausubel *et al.* (1978) argue can be exploited to facilitate the accommodation of new learning into the memory structures of the student. Both of these principles as we will see have implications for the sequencing of subject matter within a teaching sequence. The first principle is that the most general and inclusive ideas of a discipline should be presented first. These are then progressively differentiated in terms of their detail and specificity so that the most specific details are presented last. Ausubel maintains that this way of sequencing the presentation of a discipline, using the principle of progressive differentiation, parallels the way in which a student organises the content of a discipline in his own mind in the form of a hierarchical structure. The most inclusive ideas are at the apex of the hierarchy with the progressively less inclusive and more highly differentiated propositions, concepts and facts coming further down the hierarchy. Such a way of sequencing subject matter results in each level acting as a subsumer, or anchoring point, for the material which comes at the next level. In these ways, Ausubel argues, the teacher can exploit the hierarchical nature of human conceptual structures to promote optimal learning and retention.

A second principle is that new ideas should be reconciled and integrated with previously learned subject matter as soon as possible. Related ideas should be cross-referenced by the teacher whenever they occur and significant differences or similarities between ideas should be deliberately drawn to the student's attention. If the principle of integrative reconciliation is ignored, Ausubel argues, the student will be likely to use several terms for the same concept because he has not realised they are the same. Artificial barriers will be created between related topics and opportunities for gaining insights which depend upon recognising the common features between topics will be lost. The student will not be in a position to make full use of previously learned ideas to support his new learning for he will not appreciate the inter-connections between his new learning and his old. On other occasions the student may mistakenly perceive similar but none the less significantly different concepts as identical and may store them as such in his long-term memory if the teacher fails to draw the student's attention to their dissimilarities.

Ausubel's suggestions for the sequencing of subject matter are, to a very large extent, based upon much of the psychological evidence we have reviewed in earlier chapters. A learning sequence which is designed according to Ausubel's principles, taking into account the student's existing knowledge and the processes by which he will be most likely to accommodate new material efficiently into his existing conceptual structures, will differ considerably from one based exclusively upon the specialist's logical ordering of the subject matter. In place of a chain-like sequence with one idea linked progressively to the next the teacher will find himself presenting ideas in a spiral sequence.

The sequence will start with the most inclusive ideas and these ideas will be revisited in more specific detail as the teacher progresses from the advance organiser at the top of his hierarchy of concepts downwards to the increasingly detailed and specific instances. At regular intervals there will need to be opportunities for the similarities, relationships and differences between the ideas that are being presented to be explored. Such a sequence is not easy to construct but it will exploit what is known of the way in which new learning is integrated into conceptual structures in the long term memory.

Material taught in this way will have a stronger chance of being retained for long periods.

The Selection of Teaching Methods

There is no ideal method of teaching. In the previous chapter we considered some of the methods that most teachers are likely to have in their repertoire of teaching techniques. The final choice of methods that the teacher makes will depend upon the aims and objectives he has for his course, the nature of the subject matter and its sequencing, the characteristics of the students, his own skills as a teacher and the facilities which the teaching environment offers. In different contexts one factor may assume more importance than another in determining the methods that are adopted but in any choice of teaching method the teacher would do well to ensure that it will be possible for the students to be actively involved with the material that they are attempting to learn.

When a student passively listens or watches or reads there is a strong possibility that only part of the material that he should be learning will be accurately processed. With passive reception, misinterpretations can easily creep in undetected and on occasions whole sections of the material may not be satisfactorily registered in short-term memory at all. If this is the case it can only be a distorted or truncated version of the material to be learned that can go forward for storage in long-term memory.

However, if teaching methods are selected which involve appropriate student activity during the learning process, then the student will need to analyse the new material in more detail so that he can use it; as a result any misunderstandings or omissions will be more likely to become apparent. Teaching methods which require the student to recall the material actively or to express it in his own words are also likely to force him to consider the links between the new material and the other related ideas or concepts that he has already established in his conceptual structures. As we noted earlier in the chapter, new material which can be integrated into the existing conceptual structures of the learner stands the best chance of being retained in long-term memory in a stable and accurate form for a considerable period of time. More effective immediate learning and long-term retention result from teaching methods which involve the presentation and subsequent active recall of material than from methods which rely on presentation alone (Allen, Mahler and Estes, 1969; Hogan and Kintsch, 1971; Peterson, Ellis, Toohill and Kloess, 1935).

The most effective learning results from the accurate initial reception of new information, followed by active recall and use of the material in ways which force the learner to consider the interconnections between the new material and what he already knows. All the teaching methods we considered in Chapter 9 can be used in one context or another to encourage the student to integrate his new learning actively with his old.

Conclusion

In this book we have explored many of the factors which have a bearing on the way that adults learn. It is clear that in many areas our existing knowledge is at the best sketchy and imprecise. Whatever the future developments in the psychology of adult learning we can never expect to understand fully all its complexities. Psychologists make generalisations about human behaviour; they can help us to understand the characteristics that learners have in common, but every learner has special qualities of his own which make him unique. It is for this reason that although our approaches to the teaching of adults may become more scientific in the future, teaching will always remain to some extent an art.

SUGGESTED FURTHER READING

Beard, R. *Teaching and Learning in Higher Education*, 3rd edn (Penguin Books, Harmondsworth, 1976). A description of developments and innovations in teaching in higher education and a consideration of their relationship to educational theory.

Borger, R., and Seaborne, A.E.M. *The Psychology of Learning* (Penguin Books, Harmondsworth, 1966). An outline of the major psychological theories and models of learning including a consideration of their applications to formal and incidental learning.

Bromley, D.B. *The Psychology of Human Ageing*, 2nd edn (Penguin Books, Harmondsworth, 1974). An introduction to the social, psychological and behavioural aspects of ageing and their relationship to biological ageing.

Evans, P. *Motivation* (Methuen, London, 1975). A description of various theoretical approaches to the study of motivation.

Fitts, P.M., and Posner, M.I. *Human Performance* (Prentice-Hall International, London, 1973). An outline of the capacities which man brings to the performance of intellectual and physical skills. It includes a discussion of the limitations of man to attend to, process, store and transmit more than a limited amount of information.

Gagné, R.M. *The Conditions of Learning*, 3rd edn (Holt, Rinehart and Winston, New York, 1977). A full presentation with numerous illustrative examples and applications of Gagné's latest formulation of his hierarchical model of learning.

Greene, J. *Thinking and Language* (Methuen, London, 1975). A review of the different theoretical approaches to the relationship between language and thought.

Gregg, V. *Human Memory* (Methuen, London, 1975). An introduction to the psychological study of memory. The book presents recent experimental evidence whilst examining how meaning, language, imagery and events are recorded in memory.

Herriot, P. *An Introduction to the Psychology of Language* (Methuen, London, 1970). A useful survey of psychological experiments in the whole field of language.

Holding, D.H. *Principles of Training* (Pergamon Press, Oxford, 1965). A survey of some of the research on training including a consideration of its applications.

Kirby, R. and Radford, J. *Individual Differences* (Methuen, London, 1976). This book introduces some of the major problems involved in attempting to identify and assess the essential differences between people.

Krech, D., Crutchfield, R.S., and Ballachey, E.L. *Individual in Society* (McGraw-Hill, New York, 1962). Rather an old book now but still an excellent introduction to the major concepts in social psychology.

Legge, D., and Barber, P.J. *Information and Skill* (Methuen, London, 1976). This book describes the nature of the processes underlying skilled behaviour from an information processing viewpoint.

Locke, M., and Pratt, J. *A Guide to Learning After School* (Penguin Books, Harmondsworth, 1979). A guide to the variety of opportunities for post-school learning in further and higher education provided by local authorities, universities, employers, industrial training boards, government agencies, evening classes, correspondence colleges and other institutions in the United Kingdom.

Peck, D., and Whitlow, D. *Approaches to Personality Theory* (Methuen, London, 1975). A review of the major personality theories and a discussion of their applications.

Rachlin, H. *Introduction to Modern Behaviorism* (W.H. Freeman & Co., San Francisco, 1970). After describing the historical background to behaviourism, the book deals with the basic concepts in classical and operant (instrumental) conditioning and describes some of the ways in which the principles of behaviourism are being applied.

Rogers, J. *Adults Learning*, 2nd edn (Open University Press, Milton Keynes, 1977). A book intended for teachers of adults which looks at the problems actually met by adult students and goes on to consider the application of various teaching techniques. An appendix offers a useful source of information on the various agencies where the teacher of adults can obtain help.

Tajfel, H., and Fraser, C. (eds.) *Introducing Social Psychology* (Penguin Books, Harmondsworth, 1978). A general introduction to social psychology which concentrates especially on face to face interaction, attitudes and attitude change.

Thomson, R. *The Psychology of Thinking* (Penguin Books, Harmondsworth, 1959). A very readable account of many aspects of thinking including human and animal problem solving, concept attainment, motivation and learning.

Walker, S. *Learning and Reinforcement* (Methuen, London, 1975). A straightforward survey of learning theories, especially classical and operant conditioning.

Warr, P.B. (ed.) *Psychology at Work*, 2nd edn (Penguin Books, Harmondsworth, 1978). An outline of several pieces of real-life research which break down the barriers between theoretical psychology and its practical everyday applications. Many of the chapters deal with areas considered in this book.

Welford, A.T. *Fundamentals of Skill* (Methuen, London, 1968). A more advanced review of much of the psychological work on the study of skill.

BIBLIOGRAPHY

Ackerman, J.M. *Operant Conditioning Techniques for the Classroom Teacher* (Scott, Foresman & Co., Illinois, 1972).

Adams, J.A. 'A Closed-loop Theory of Motor Learning', *Journal of Motor Behavior,* vol. 3, no. 2 (1971), pp. 111-49.

Allen, G.A., Mahler, W.A., and Estes, W.K. 'Effects of Recall Tests on Long-term Retention of Paired Associates', *Journal of Verbal Learning and Verbal Behavior,* vol. 8 (1969), p. 463-70.

Anderson, R.C. 'Learning in Discussions: a Resume of the Authoritarian-Democratic Studies', *Harvard Educational Review,* vol. 29 (1959), pp. 201-15.

Arenberg, D. 'A Longitudinal Study of Problem Solving in Adults', *Journal of Gerontology,* vol. 29 (1974), pp. 650-8.

Ausubel, D.P., Novak, J.D., and Hanesian, H. *Educational Psychology: A Cognitive View,* 2nd edn (Holt, Rinehart and Winston, New York, 1978).

Ayllon, T., and Azrin, N.H. *The Token Economy: A Motivational System for Therapy and Rehabilitation* (Appleton-Century-Crofts, New York, 1968).

Backman, C.W., and Secord, P.F. *A Social Psychological View of Education* (Harcourt Brace, New York, 1968).

Bales, R.F. and Slater, P.E. 'Role Differentiation in Small Decision Making Groups', in Parsons, T., and Bales, R.F. (eds.) *Family, Socialization and Interaction Process* (Free Press, New York, 1955), Chapter 5.

Bartlett, F.C. *Remembering* (Cambridge University Press, Cambridge, 1932).

Bayley, N. and Oden, M.H. 'The Maintenance of Intellectual Ability in Gifted Adults', *Journal of Gerontology,* vol. 10 (1955), pp. 91-107.

Beard, R. *Teaching and Learning in Higher Education,* 3rd edn (Penguin Books, Harmondsworth, 1976).

Beard, R.M., Bligh, D.A., and Harding, A.G. *Research into Teaching Methods in Higher Education,* 4th edn (Society for Research into Higher Education, University of Surrey, 1978).

Belbin, E. 'Training the Adult Worker', *Problems of Progress in Industry,* no. 15 (HMSO, 1964).

148

Belbin, R.M. *Employment of Older Workers: Training Methods* (OECD Publications, Paris, 1965).

Berlyne, D.E. *Conflict, Arousal and Curiosity* (McGraw Hill, New York, 1960).

Bexton, W.H., Heron, W., and Scott, T.H. 'Effects of Decreased Variation in the Sensory Environment' *Canadian Journal of Psychology,* vol. 8 (1954), pp. 70-6.

Birch, H.G. 'The Relation of Previous Experience to Insightful Problem Solving', *Journal of Comparative Psychology*, vol. 38 (1945) pp. 367-83.

Birch, H.G., and Rabinowitz, H.S. 'The Negative Effect of Previous Experience on Productive Thinking', *Journal of Experimental Psychology,* vol. 41 (1951), pp. 121-5.

Birren, J.E. *The Psychology of Aging* (Prentice-Hall, Englewood Cliffs, New Jersey, 1964).

Bligh D.A. *What's the Use of Lectures?* (Penguin Books, Harmondsworth, 1972).

Bloom, B.S. (ed.) *Taxonomy of Educational Objectives Handbook: Cognitive Domain* (McKay, New York, 1956).

Blum, J.E., and Jarvik, L.F. 'Intellectual Performance of Octogenarians as a Function of Educational and Initial Ability', *Human Development*, vol. 17 (1974), pp. 364-75.

Bousefield, W.A. 'The Occurrence of Clustering in the Recall of Randomly Arranged Associates,' *Journal of General Psychology,* vol. 49 (1953), pp. 229-40.

Bromley, D.B. *The Psychology of Human Ageing*, 2nd edn (Penguin Books, Harmondsworth, 1974).

Brown, I.D. 'Measuring the Spare Mental Capacity of Car Drivers by a Subsidiary Auditory Task', *Ergonomics*, vol. 5 (1962), pp. 247-50.

Bruner, J.S., Goodnow, J.J., and Austin, G.A. *A Study of Thinking* (John Wiley & Sons, New York, 1956).

Butcher, H.J. *Human Intelligence* (Methuen, London, 1968).

Cattell, R.B. 'Theory of Fluid and Crystallized Intelligence: A Critical Experiment,' *Journal of Educational Psychology*, vol. 54 (1963), pp. 1-22.

Collins, A.M., and Quillian, M.R. 'Retrieval Time from Semantic Memory', *Journal of Verbal Learning and Verbal Behavior*, vol. 8 (1969), pp. 240-7.

Cooley, C.H. *Human Nature and the Social Order* (Charles Scribner's Sons, New York, 1902).

—— *Social Organisation* (Charles Scribner's Sons, New York, 1909).

Craik, F.I.M., and Lockhart, R.S. 'Levels of Processing: A Framework for Memory Research', *Journal of Verbal Learning and Verbal Behavior*, vol. 11 (1972), pp. 671-84.

Cunningham, W.R., and Birren, J.E. 'Age Changes in Human Abilities: a 28-year Longitudinal Study', *Developmental Psychology*, vol. 12, no. 1 (1976), pp. 81-2.

Duncker, K. 'On Problem Solving', *Psychological Monographs*, vol. 58, no. 270 (1945).

Evans, D. 'The Effects of Achievement Motivation and Ability upon Discovery Learning and Accompanying Incidental Learning under Two Conditions of Incentive Set', *Journal of Educational Research*, vol. 60, no. 5 (1967), pp. 195-200.

Eysenck, H.J. *Sense and Nonsense in Psychology* (Penguin Books, Harmondsworth, 1957).

—— *The Biological Basis of Personality* (Thomas, Springfield, 1967).

—— *The Structure of Human Personality* (University of London Press, London, 1960).

Festinger, L. 'A Theory of Social Comparison Processes' *Human Relations*, (1954), pp. 117-40.

Festinger, L., Schacter, S., and Back, K. *Social Pressures in Informal Groups* (Harper & Row, New York, 1950).

Fiedler, F. 'Leader Attitudes, Group Climate and Group Activity', *Journal of Social and Abnormal Psychology*, vol. 65 (1962).

—— 'The Contingency Model: a Theory of Leadership Effectiveness' in Proshansky, H. and Seidenberg, B. (eds.) *Basic Studies in Social Psychology* (Holt, Rinehart and Winston, New York, 1965).

Foulds, G.A. 'Mill Hill Vocabulary and Matrices', *American Journal of Psychology*, vol. 62 (1949), pp. 238-46.

Foulds, G.A., and Raven, J.C. 'Neural Changes in Mental Abilities of Adults as Age Advances', *Journal of Mental Science*, vol. 94 (1948), pp. 133-42.

Freedman, M.B. *The Student and Campus Climates of Learning* (US Department of Health, Education and Welfare, Washington, D.C., 1967).

Gagne, R.M. *The Conditions of Learning*, 3rd edn (Holt, Rinehart and Winston, New York, 1977).

Ginsburg, G.P., and Whittlemore, R.G.'Creativity and Verbal Ability:

A Direct Examination of their Relationship', *British Journal of Educational Psychology*, vol. 38 (1968), pp. 133-9.

Green, R.F. 'Age-Intelligence Relationships between Ages Sixteen and Sixty-four: A Rising Trend', *Developmental Psychology*, vol. 1 (1969), pp. 618-27.

Gregg, V. *Human Memory* (Methuen, London, 1975).

Gronlund, N.E. *Measurement and Evaluation in Teaching*, 3rd edn (Macmillan Publishing Co., New York, 1976).

Grotelueschen, A., and Sjorgren, D.D. 'Effects of Differentially Structured Introductory Materials and Learning Tasks on Learning and Transfer', *American Educational Research Journal*, vol. 5 (1968), pp. 191-202.

Guilford, J.P. 'The Structure of Intellect', *Psychological Bulletin*, vol. 53 (1956), pp. 267-93.

Hall, C.S., and Lindzey, G. *Theories of Personality*, 2nd edn (John Wiley & Sons, New York, 1970).

Harlow, H.F. 'The Formation of Learning Sets', *Psychological Review*, no. 56 (1949), pp. 51-65.

Hebb, D.O. *The Organization of Behavior* (John Wiley & Sons, New York, 1949).

Hill, J. 'The Psychological Impact of Unemployment', *New Society*, 19 Jan. 1978.

Hogan, R.M., and Kintsch, W. 'Differential Effects of Study and Test Trials on Long-term Retention and Recall', *Journal of Verbal Learning and Verbal Behavior*, vol. 10 (1971), pp. 562-7.

Homans, G.C. 'Social Behavior as Exchange', *American Journal of Sociology*, vol. 63 (1958).

Howarth, E., and Eysenck, H.J. 'Extraversion, Arousal, and Paired-associate Recall', *Journal of Experimental Research in Personality*, vol. 3 (1968), pp. 114-16.

Huckabee, M.W. 'Introversion-Extraversion and Imagery', *Psychological Reports*, vol. 34 (1974), pp. 453-4.

Hudson, L. *Contrary Imaginations: A Psychological Study of the English Schoolboy* (Methuen, London, 1966).

—— *Frames of Mind: Ability, Perception and Self-perception in the Arts and Sciences* (Methuen, London, 1968).

Jerome, E.A. 'Decay of Heuristic Processes in the Aged' in Tibbitts, C., and Donahue, W. (eds.) *Social and Psychological Aspects of Aging* (Columbia University Press, New York, 1962).

Jones, H.A. 'What Do They Expect?' in Rogers, J. (ed.) *Teaching on Equal Terms* (BBC Publications, London, 1969).

Josephs A.P., and Smithers, A.G. 'Personality Characteristics of Syllabus-bound and Syllabus-free Sixth-formers', *British Journal of Educational Psychology*, vol. 45 (1975), pp. 29-38.

Kagan, J. 'Impulsive and Reflective Children: Significance of Conceptual Tempo', in *Learning and the Educational Process* (Rand McNally, Chicago, 1965), pp. 133-61.

Keys, A. 'Experimental Introduction of Psychoneuroses by Starvation', The Biology of Mental Health and Disease, 27th Annual Conference: Milbank Memorial Fund (Harper & Row, New York, 1952).

Knox, A.B., Grotelueschen, A.D., and Sjorgren, D.D. 'Adult Intelligence and Learning Ability', *Adult Education*, vol. 18, no. 3 (1968), pp. 188-96.

Köhler, W. *The Mentality of Apes* (Routledge & Kegan Paul, London 1925 and Penguin Books, Harmondsworth, 1957).

Krathwohl, D.R., Bloom, B.S., and Masia, B.B. *Taxonomy of Educational Objectives, Handbook II: Affective Domain* (McKay, New York, 1964).

Krech, D., Crutchfield, R.S., and Ballachey, E.L. *Individual in Society* (McGraw Hill, New York, 1962).

Kuhn, D.J., and Novak, J.D. 'A Study of Cognitive Subsumption in the Life Sciences', *Science Education*, vol. 55 (1971), pp. 309-20.

Kuhn, H.H. 'Self Attitudes by Age, Sex, and Professional Training', *Sociological Quarterly*, vol. 1 (1960), pp. 39-55.

Legge, D., and Barber, P.L. *Information and Skill* (Methuen, London, 1976).

Leith, G., Lister, A., Teall, C., and Bellingham, J. 'Teaching the New Decimal Currency by Programmed Instruction', *Industrial Training International*, vol. 3 (1968), pp 424-7.

Lewin, K., Lippitt, R., and White, R.K. 'Patterns of Aggressive Behavior in Experimentally Created "Social Climates"', *Journal of Social Psychology*, vol. 10 (1939), pp. 271-99.

Longley, C. (ed.) *Games and Simulations* (BBC Publications, London, 1972).

Luchins, A.S. 'Mechanisation in Problem Solving: the Effect of Einstellung', *Psychological Monographs*, vol. 54, no. 248 (1942), pp. 1-95.

McClelland, D.C., Atkinson, J.W., Clark, R.A., and Lowell, E.L. *The Achievement Motive* (Appleton-Century-Crofts, New York, 1953).

MacKinnon, D.W. 'The Personality Correlates of Creativity:A Study of American Architects' in *Proceedings of the Fourteenth Congress of Applied Psychology*, vol. 2 (1962), pp. 11-39 in Vernon, P.E. (ed), *Creativity* (Penguin Books, Harmondsworth, 1970).

McMurray, D.W., and Duffy, T.M. 'Meaningfulness and Pronounce-ability as Chunking Units in Short-term Memory', *Journal of Experimental Psychology*, vol. 96 (1972), pp. 291-6.

Mager, R.F. 'On the Sequencing of Instructional Content', *Psychological Reports*, vol. 9 (1961), pp. 405-13.

—— *Preparing Instructional Objectives* (Fearon Publishers, Belmont, California, 1962).

Mager, R.F., and Clark, C. 'Explorations in Student-controlled Instruction', *Psychological Reports*, vol. 13 (1963), pp. 71-6.

Mager, R.F., and McCann, J. *Learner-controlled Instruction* (Varian Associates, Palo Alto, 1963).

Maier, N.R.F. 'Reasoning in Humans: III. The Mechanisms of Equivalent Stimuli and of Reasoning', *Journal of Experimental Psychology*, vol. 35 (1945), pp. 349-60.

Maizels, J. *Adolescent Needs and the Transition from School to Work* (Athlone Press, London, 1970).

Maslow, A.H. 'A Theory of Human Motivation', *Psychological Review*, vol. 50 (1943), pp. 370-96.

—— *Towards a Psychology of Being*, 2nd edn (Van Nostrand, Princeton, New Jersey, 1968).

Mead, G.H. *Mind, Self and Society from the Standpoint of a Social Behaviorist* (University of Chicago Press, 1934).

Miller, R.B. *Handbook on Training and Training Equipment Design* (WADC, Tech. Report 53-136, US Air Force, 1953).

Miller, G.A. 'The Magical Number Seven, Plus or Minus Two: Some Limits on Our Capacity for Processing Information', *Psychological Review*, vol. 63 (1956), pp. 81-97.

Miller, G.A., Galanter, E., and Pribram, K.M. *Plans and the Structure of Behavior* (Holt, Rinehart and Winston, New York, 1960).

Morstain, B.R., and Smart, J.C. 'A Motivational Typology of Adult Learners', *Journal of Higher Education*, vol. 48, no. 6 (1978), pp. 665-79.

Newcomb, T.M. *The Acquaintance Process* (Holt, Rinehart and Winston, New York, 1961).

Newsham, D.B. *The Challenge of Change to the Adult Trainee* (Training Information Pamphlet no. 3, HMSO, London, 1969).

Parlett, M.R. 'The Syllabus-bound Student' (Research Report,

Education Research Center, Massachusetts Institute of Technology, 1969) in Hudson, L. (ed.) *The Ecology of Human Intelligence* (Penguin Books, Harmondsworth, 1970).

Pask, G. 'Strategy, Competence and Conversation as Determinants of Learning', *Programmed Learning* (Oct. 1969), p. 250.

Peterson, H.A., Ellis, M., Toohill N., and Kloess, P. 'Some Measurements of the Effects of Reviews', *Journal of Educational Psychology*, vol. 26 (1935), pp. 65-72.

Pew, R.W. 'Acquisition of Hierarchical Control over the Temporal Acquisition of a Skill', *Journal of Experimental Psychology*, vol. 71 (1966), pp. 764-71.

Piaget, J. *The Psychology of Intelligence* (Routledge & Kegan Paul, London, 1950).

Polya, G. *How to Sòlve It* (Princeton University Press, 1945).

Roberts, D.M. 'Abilities and Learning: A Brief Review and Discussion of Empirical Studies', *Journal of School Psychology*, vol. 7 (1968), pp. 12-21.

Rokeach, M. *The Open and Closed Mind* (Basic Books, New York, 1960).

Saugstad, P. and Raaheim, B.K. 'Problem Solving, Past Experience and Availability of Function', *British Journal of Psychology*, vol. 51 (1960), pp. 97-104.

Schachter, S. 'Deviation, Rejection and Communication,' *Journal of Abnormal and Social Psychology*, vol. 46 (1951), pp. 190-207.

—— *The Psychology of Affiliation* (Stanford University Press, 1959).

Schmuck, R. 'Some Aspects of Classroom Social Climate', *Psychology in the Schools*, vol. 3, no. 1 (1966), pp. 59-65.

Schonell, F.J., Roe, E., and Middleton, I.G. *Promise and Performance* (University of Queensland Press, 1962).

Schvanevelat, R.W. 'Concept Identification as a Function of Probability of Positive Instances and Number of Relevant Dimensions', *Journal of Experimental Psychology*, vol. 72 (1966), pp. 649-60.

Shadbolt, D.R., and Leith, G.O.M. *Mode of Learning and Personality II. Research Reports on Programmed Learning* (University of Birmingham, 1967).

Shooter, A.M.N. *et al.* 'Some Field Data on the Training of Older People', *Occupational Psychology*, vol. 30 (1956), pp. 204-15.

Simon, H.A. *The Sciences of the Artificial* (MIT Press, Cambridge, Mass., 1969).

Skinner, B.F. *Beyond Freedom and Dignity* (Knopf, New York,

1971).

—— *Cumulative Record*, 3rd edn (Appleton-Century-Crofts, New York, 1972).

Sperling, G. 'The Information Available in a Brief Visual Presentation', *Psychological Monographs*, vol. 74, no. 498 (1960).

Taylor, J.L., and Walford, R. *Simulation in the Classroom* (Penguin Books, Harmondsworth, 1972).

Thibaut, J.W. , and Kelley, H.H. *The Social Psychology of Groups* (John Wiley & Sons, New York, 1959).

Thorndike, E.L. 'Animal Intelligence', *Psych. Rev. Monograph* vol. 2, no. 8 (1898).

—— 'The Law of Effect', *Americal Journal of Psychology*, vol. 39 (1927), pp. 212-22.

Thyne, J.M. *Principles of Examining* (University of London Press, 1974).

Vernon, P.E. 'The Assessment of Children', in *Studies in Education* (University of London Institute of Education, 1955), pp. 189-215.

Ward, I. 'The Apportionment of Time by College Students', *The Vocational Aspect of Education*, vol. 25, no. 62 (1973), pp. 133-7.

Wechsler, D. *The Measurement and Appraisal of Adult Intelligence*, 3rd edn (Williams & Wilkins, Baltimore, 1958).

Welford, A.T. *Ageing and Human Skill* (Oxford University Press, 1958).

——'Changes in Speed of Performance with Age and their Individual Significance', *Ergonomics*, vol. 5 (1962), pp. 139-45.

—— *Fundamentals of Skill* (Methuen, London, 1968).

Wertheimer, M. *Productive Thinking*, enlarged edn (Tavistock Publications, London, 1961).

Winch, R.F., Ktsanes, T., and Ktsanes, V. 'Empirical Elaboration of the Theory of Complementary Needs in Mate-selection', *Journal of Abnormal and Social Psychology*, vol. 51 (1955), pp. 508-13.

Winterbottom, M.R. 'The Relation of Childhood Training in Independence to Achievement Motivation, University of Michigan, cited in D.C. McClelland *et al.* (1953).

Witkin, H.A., 'Some Implications of Research on Cognitive Style for Problems of Education', in Gottesgen, M.B., and Gottesgen, G.B. (eds.) *Professional School Psychology* vol. 3 (Grune & Stratton), New York, 1969), pp. 198-227.

Witkin, H.A., Lewis, H.B., Hertzman, M., Machover, K., Meissener P.B., and Wapner, S. *Personality Through Perception* (Harper &

Row, New York, 1954).

Yamamoto, K. 'Effects of Restriction of Range and Test Reliability on Correlation between Measures of Intelligence and Creative Thinking', *British Journal of Educational Psychology*, vol. 35 (1965), pp. 300-5.

GLOSSARY

Accommodation. The integration of new knowledge with existing knowledge in the conceptual structures of the individual's long-term memory.

Advance Organiser. Provides a scaffolding of ideas which bridge the gap between what a student already knows and what he needs to know before he can learn new material in a meaningful fashion. Such a scaffolding should consist of a stable cognitive structure of high level ideas which can be used to incorporate the more detailed and specific information which will follow.

Affiliative Needs. Most people have a need to feel that they belong together with others. This need may well have its origins in the satisfactions that we obtained when we were totally dependent for our survival upon the support of the family group.

Association. A connection between two or more sensations, ideas or images.

Attitudes. Have their origins in our past social experiences and they very largely determine our future responses to the social objects with which they are connected. They are similar to a 'set' in problem solving. Attitudes affect our perception and interpretation of social situations very strongly and hence determine how we will respond. Attitudes have cognitive, affective (emotional) and action tendency aspects. Attitudes often cluster together to produce an attitude system.

Autonomic Nervous System. A subdivision of the nervous system which innervates the glands and involuntary muscles. Amongst other things it controls the physiological changes that occur in the body during different emotional states.

Available Functions. The possible range of uses for an object that we have available in our mind. These will vary for individuals depending upon their past experiences with the objects.

Behaviour. Any action or actions of the individual.

Behaviourism. A branch of psychology which attempts to discover the laws that describe behaviour by relying exclusively on observable data.

Classical Conditioning. The learning that occurs as the result of a pairing of a neutral stimulus with a stimulus correlated with a reflexive response. An individual who experiences repeated pairings of this kind may learn to respond to the neutral stimulus in the way that is appropriate to the other stimulus.

Closed-loop Control. In skilled behaviour this occurs much of the time. An individual response is made, the feedback or information about the consequence of the response is analysed and an appropriate subsequent response is then made. This response in its turn generates feedback which is analysed and a further correction is initiated and so on. In a highly skilled operator an open-loop system of control may be adapted from time to time.

Cognitive Learning. Learning that is concerned with the various aspects of knowing such as perception, memory, imagination, judgement, reasoning and problem solving.

Concept. A system of learned responses which enables us to organise and interpret data. Concepts are usually associated with specific words or phrases but we can have an idea of a class of objects without verbal labels to identify them.

Conceptual Structure. Concepts become linked with others in various ways. Within the mind of the individual, concepts become organised together to produce a hierarchical network of concepts. The nature of the network of interrelated concepts will vary from individual to individual depending upon their previous experiences.

Conditioned Response. The new response to the previously neutral stimulus which is learned as a result of classical conditioning. It is often very similar to the unconditioned response originally produced to the unconditioned stimulus.

Conditioned Stimulus. Stimulus which is originally neutral but which comes to elicit a conditioned response as a result of its repeated pairing with an unconditioned stimulus that normally produces the response.

Convergent Thinking. A cognitive operation in which the information given leads the subject to a right or conventional 'best' answer. It is often contrasted with divergent thinking.

Crystallised Intelligence. The result of fluid intelligence being mixed with cultural knowledge. It is known as crystallised because it is a precipitate out of experience. It increases with the individual's experience and formal education. It is most evident in activities such as general information, verbal comprehension, coping with social situations and arithmetical reasoning.

Divergent Thinking. A cognitive operation in which the subject thinks in different directions. The quality of divergent thought is judged in terms of the quantity, variety and originality of the ideas produced. It is often contrasted with convergent thinking.

Environment. All the stimuli which impinge upon the individual; they may be external or internal to the individual in their origins.

Exchange Theory. An approach that looks upon social behaviour in terms of its costs and benefits. It is suggested a person will maintain social interaction with another if the profit from the interaction satisfies the individual's expectation and it is more profitable than any alternative social interaction that is available. Profitability may relate to obtaining primary needs or social reinforcements. The costs may include fatigue, boredom, increased anxiety, embarrassment or the loss or prestige or reputation.

Extinction. The elimination of the learned response in both classical and operant conditioning.

Extravert. A very social and outgoing person. He is impulsive and tends to do things on the spur of the moment. He likes plenty of action in his world. His emotions are often given free play, he is quick to lose his temper and is not especially reliable. He is more difficult to classically condition than the introvert.

Extrinsic Feedback. Feedback about one's performance of a skill, provided by a teacher or instructor.

Feedback. Information about the consequences of the actions taken by a person performing a skill. The information may be internal, coming from within the performer through the kinaesthetic sense receptors, or it may be external in its origins and come through the senses of sight, hearing, touch, taste or smell.

Field-dependent. A term used to describe a subject who relies on external cues rather than his internal proprioceptive sense receptors in judging his relationship to the environment. Often contrasted with field-independent.

Field-independent. A term used to describe a subject who relies exclusively on his own internal sensory process in judging his relationship to the environment. Often contrasted with field-dependent.

Fluid Intelligence. This is involved in our ability to perceive complex relationships, to recognise and retain an awareness of the immediate environment as in short-term memory, to form concepts and to engage in abstract reasoning. It is rather formless and relatively independent of education and experience. It can 'flow' into a wide range of activities and interacts with experience to form crystallised intelligence.

Formal Learning. Learning where there is a teacher who is responsible for directing the learner's progress usually in relation to a syllabus or pre-arranged programme.

Functional Fixedness. The inability to see the full range of potential uses for an object. The previous uses of the object become fixed in the mind as the only uses to which the object can be put.

Generalisation. In both classical and operant conditioning, generalisation occurs when the individual produces learned responses to stimuli similar but not identical to those used in the original conditioning.

Group Cohesiveness. A measure of the degree of unity amongst group members. A highly cohesive group typically has a high level of mutual attraction amongst group members, members share attitudes in matters that relate to the group, the group structure is well developed and accepted and the members are clear about their group roles. There is a strong degree of conformity to group norms and there is likely to be a stable and long lasting membership.

Holist. A subject who remembers and recalls material he is studying as a whole. He attempts to gain an overview of an area of study so that the detail can fall into place. He is often contrasted with the serialist.

Impulsivity. The tendency in some subjects to blurt out possible answers to problems in rapid succession without due consideration of all the possible evidence contributing to a solution. The impulsive subject often relies on an external source such as a teacher to evaluate the quality of his responses. Often contrasted with reflectivity.

Incidental Learning. Learning that is not deliberately undertaken but which occurs as a consequence of day to day activities.

Insight. The sudden awareness of the interrelationship between parts of a problem leading to a solution which results from the restructuring of the elements of the problem in a new way.

Integrative reconciliation. The principle that when teaching new ideas they should be reconciled and integrated with previously learned subject matter as soon as possible. Wherever possible similar ideas should be cross-referenced as soon as possible and significant differences between superficially similar ideas should be drawn to students' attention.

Intrinsic Feedback. Feedback that comes from the performance of a skill rather than from the assessment made by a teacher or instructor.

Introvert. A rather quiet, shy and private person who likes to plan ahead and has his emotions under fairly tight control. Life for him is a serious affair and he tends to take a rather pessimistic view. He is reliable and sets himself high ethical standards. He is more easily classically conditioned than an extravert.

Kinaesthetic Sense. The sense which provides us with information from within our body about the movement of our body and limbs. The carefully controlled physical movements characteristic of so many skills are controlled by the proprioceptive information provided by our kinaesthetic sense receptors which are located in nerve endings in muscles, tendons and joints.

Knowledge of Results. A form of feedback which enables us to identify what effect our actions have had when we are carrying out a skill.

Learning. The relatively permanent changes in potential for performance that result from past interactions with the environment.

Long-term Memory. Part of the memory system with unlimited capacity where information is often stored for indefinite lengths of time. Material stored in long-term memory is not always easy to recall to conscious attention.

Meaningful Learning. Learning which can be related to existing aspects of the learner's conceptual structure.

Motivation. That which directs an individual's behaviour towards the satisfaction of some need.

Norms. The expectations held by group members about the ways members should behave in connection with matters that affect the group. They may be formally stated as, for example, rules, or tacitly accepted by members of the group.

Open-loop Control. As the individual becomes more competent at a skill, the movement patterns that have been well practised become represented centrally in the brain or spinal cord in some fashion. This programme for controlling the physical actions involved in performing the skill may be played off like a tape or record without the need for modification from the feedback which occurs with a closed-loop system of control. As we become more skilled we move from a closed-loop to at least a partially open-loop system of control.

Operant conditioning. (Also called Instrumental conditioning). This involves establishing a relationship between some form of behaviour and reinforcement or punishment. The individual has been operantly conditioned when he modifies his behaviour to obtain the reinforcement or to avoid the punishment.

Personality. The relatively stable ways of responding towards the world that typifies the behaviour of a particular individual. In some ways the behaviour of the individual is like that of all other people, in some ways it is like that of some other people, in some ways it is unique to the individual. Different theories of personality concentrate more on one of these aspects of behaviour than on the others.

Plan. Any hierarchical process that can control the order in which a sequence of behavioural operations is carried out. Plans are involved in the performance of skills as well as in the more obviously cognitive activities such as problem solving.

Primary Group. A social group which is small enough for all its members to be involved in face to face interaction and which involves the individual fully in mutual identification with other group members. Typical examples are the family unit and the immediate work group.

Problem Solving. The process through which the learner draws upon his repertoire of previously learned responses to find a solution to a new problem.

Productive thought. One of the two major strategies (the other is reproductive thought) employed in problem solving. A solution to a problem is reached by repatterning and restructuring past experience in order to meet the special circumstances of the problem. No rules are available to assist productive thought. When a successful solution has been reached it will be stored as a rule for possible future use in reproductive thought.

Progressive Differentiation. When planning the sequencing of subject matter the principle of progressive differentiation suggests that the most general and inclusive ideas of a discipline should be presented first. The ideas can then be steadily made more detailed and specific with the most specific details being presented last.

Proprioceptive Information. Sensory information that comes from the kinaesthetic sense receptors that are located within the body in muscles, tendons and joints. Such information enables us to tell when, as a result of a muscular change, a movement has been made or pressure exerted.

Reference Group. When an individual identifies with the goals and norms of a group and adopts the values and attitudes of its members it becomes a reference group for the individual. It is not necessary to be a member of a group for it to act as a reference group.

Adolescents, for example, often identify with groups that they would like to join.

Reflectivity. The tendency in some people to delay a long time until they are certain of the correctness of their response before venturing an answer to a problem. Such subjects seem to have a strong desire to be right the first time and can tolerate the long pauses often necessary to evaluate for themselves the response they are considering giving. Often contrasted with impulsivity.

Reinforcement. In operant conditioning the presentation of a 'reward' (positive reinforcement) or the removal of an aversive stimulus (negative reinforcement). In classical conditioning reinforcement is produced by the repeated pairings of the unconditioned and conditioned stimuli.

Reproductive Thought. One of the two major strategies (the other is productive thought) employed in problem solving. A solution to a problem is reached through the direct application of strategies and approaches which are already familiar from previous learning. Similar to transfer of training, reproductive thought involves the application of already learned rules.

Response. Any action of the individual, either neural, muscular or glandular which results from some form of stimulation.

Reticular System. Sensory nerves from different parts of the body supply the cortex or outer layer of the brain directly. They also send branches to the reticular system which cause the cortex to become generally aroused when there is sensory stimulation reaching it. The system continues to maintain the arousal of the cortex whilst stimulation persists and this we recognise as attention.

Role. Groups usually require a division of labour or function between group members in order to best achieve the ends of the group. A role represents the behaviour that is expected of a group member depending upon his status or position in the power structure of the group. The norms of the group will help determine how the individual should play his role. The roles of group members are interdependent.

Rote Learning. Occurs when material is learned by heart in a parrot fashion without it being related in any meaningful way to the learner's existing conceptual structures.

Rule. The existence of a rule can be inferred when the individual responds to a class of stimulus situations with a class of performances. Rules can determine the way that we will behave even though we cannot consciously identify them.

Schema. (Plural schemata.) A mental framework which results from previous experience and is used to process new experiences. Sometimes important detail may be omitted from the recollection of a new experience if it doesn't fit readily into an existing schema. An aspect of the 'filing system' of the memory.

Secondary Group. A social group which involves a contractual association between its members for the achievement of very specific goals. We may never meet many of our fellow members in a secondary group; those we do encounter we relate to in a rather formal and impersonal way and only a small part of our total personality is likely to be involved. Typical examples of a secondary group are a trade union or a charitable organisation.

Self Actualisation. The fulfilment of one's potentialities. Successful self actualisation depends upon being able to recognise one's own capabilities.

Self-concept. This has three main elements: (i) the self-image or the impression we hold of ourselves — this is constructed largely from the way we think we see ourselves reflected back from the minds of others; (ii) the ideal self or the image of the way we could be or ought to be or would like to be and (iii) self-esteem or the feelings we have about the self we believe ourselves to be.

Semantic Level of Analysis. Analysis of verbal material in terms of the meanings of the words. This meaning may be in terms of other defining words as well as in terms of visual images.

Sensori-motor Skills. Skills which involve both the reception and processing of information from the senses as well as the production of physical or motor responses.

Sensory Memory. The first stage in memory where the effect of sensory stimulation is held in storage for a brief moment after it has been experienced. The effect of this stimulation is either lost or transferred to short-term memory.

Serialist. A subject who approaches the study of new material by stringing a sequence of cognitive structures together. He is intolerant of redundant information in his learning because of the extra burden this imposes on memory. He prefers to build up a total picture by stringing detail together. He is often contrasted with the holist.

Set. A predisposition, as a result of previous experience, to behave in a particular way. A set reduces the necessity to make decisions about how to behave when we are faced with familiar situations. It can lead to the production of an inappropriate stereotyped response.

Shaping. In operant conditioning when the desired response is slow to appear, responses that resemble the desired behaviour at least in part are reinforced. Gradually the criterion for reinforced behaviour is shifted from the approximation closer and closer to the desired response.

Short-term Memory. (Working memory.) Part of the memory system where a limited amount of information can be held briefly in storage for immediate use. Coded information can increase its capacity for storage. Information in short-term memory will be rapidly lost unless it is rehearsed or goes forward to long-term memory.

Social Climate. In an organisation the social climate results from an interaction between organisational factors and the personality characteristics of the members of the organisation.

Socialisation. The process by which an individual comes to accept the attitudes, values and norms of the social groups of which he is a member. The process of socialisation begins in the family and continues throughout our lives as we come under the influence of new groups and as the norms of society change.

Socio-emotional Leader. One who takes on the role of maintaining the unity and good morale within a group by improving communications between group members and by helping to reduce the friction and tension within the group that is sometimes created by a task leader.

Spontaneous Recovery. In both operant and classical conditioning learned responses which have been extinguished may reappear in the individual's repertoire of behaviour at a later date without any further reinforcement. Such responses are said to have spontaneously recovered.

Status. Each group has its own structure of power. The status of group members is an indication of where they are placed in the pecking order. Members with high status usually have considerable control over the way ideas and information are communicated within the group. The status of the individual will determine his influence in setting the group norms and will also influence the way he plays his role.

Stimulus. Any environmental event that has an effect on the individual.

Strategy. A plan of action.

Sylb. A subject who is syllabus-bound in his approach to study. The typical sylb is almost exclusively concerned with getting good examination marks and happily accepts the restrictions on his approaches to study produced by a formal syllabus. He is often contrasted with the sylf.

Sylf. A subject who is syllabus-free. The typical sylf has intellectual interests that extend far beyond the syllabus and often has difficulty in confining his study to the requirements of a formal syllabus. He is often contrasted with the sylb.

Syntactic Level of Analysis. Analysis of verbal material in terms of the grammatical functions of the words rather than in terms of their meanings.

Task Leader. A group member who takes on the role of recognising and diagnosing the problems that stand between a group and the realisation of its objectives. He often initiates, plans and directs the group in such a way that members may on occasions need to modify their behaviour within the group. Any tensions that this sets up may be released by a socio-emotional leader.

Transfer of Training. The measure of the extent to which a skill learned in one context can be successfully applied in another somewhat different context. It may be either positive or negative. Positive transfer occurs, for example, when the original learning makes it easier for the individual to master a new but related skill; negative transfer occurs when the previous learning makes it more difficult for a new skill to be mastered.

Unconditioned Response. The response to the unconditioned stimulus that normally occurs and which becomes attached to the conditioned stimulus as a result of its repeated pairing with the unconditioned stimulus during classical conditioning.

Unconditioned Stimulus. The stimulus which normally produces the specific unconditioned reflexive response involved in a classical conditioning situation before the learning takes place.

INDEX

167